Eden's Bounty

By
Diana Inman, CDA
Ruth Abbott, PhD, RN

www.TEACHServices.com • (800) 367-1844

World rights reserved. This book or any portion thereof may not be copied or reproduced in any form or manner whatever, except as provided by law, without the written permission of the publisher, except by a reviewer who may quote brief passages in a review.

This book was written to provide truthful information in regard to the subject matter covered. The author assumes full responsibility for the accuracy of all facts and quotations as cited in this book. The opinions expressed in this book are the author's personal views and interpretation of the Bible, Spirit of Prophecy, and/or contemporary authors and do not necessarily reflect those of TEACH Services, Inc.

This book is sold with the understanding that the publisher is not engaged in giving spiritual, legal, medical, or other professional advice. If authoritative advice is needed, the reader should seek the counsel of a competent professional.

Copyright © 2013 TEACH Services, Inc.
ISBN-13: 978-1-4796-0230-8 (Paperback)
ISBN-13: 978-1-4796-0231-5 (ePub)
ISBN-13: 978-1-4796-0232-2 (Kindle/Mobi)

Library of Congress Control Number: 2013940982

Published by

www.TEACHServices.com • (800) 367-1844

Appreciation

We want to express our appreciation to our families and friends who have helped to make this book possible. Also to those who have attended our cooking classes, who not only tasted and critiqued our many recipes, but who also motivated us to create this cookbook. We hope that this collection of recipes and natural remedies will bless those who use them. Finally, we wish to give the glory to God, because without Him nothing is possible.

*"Whatsoever your hand finds to do,
do it with all your might."*

Ecclesiastes 9:10

*"Bless the Lord, O my soul,
and forget not all his benefits.
Who forgiveth all thine iniquities;
who healeth all thy diseases;
Who redeemeth thy life from destruction;
who crowneth thee with loving kindness
and tender mercies;
Who satisfieth thy mouth with good things;
so that thy youth is renewed
like the eagle's."*

Psalms 103:2–5

Contents

Breakfast 9

Breads & Spreads 17

Soups 27

Salads & Vegetables 33

Main Dishes 43

Desserts 55

This & That 65

Herbs & Natural Remedies 81

Miscellaneous 120

Index 122

"Taste and see that the Lord is good;
blessed is the man who takes refuge in Him."

—Psalms 34:8

Breakfast

"Let the table be made inviting and attractive,
as it is supplied with the good things which God
has bountifully bestowed. Let mealtime be a cheerful,
happy time. As we enjoy the gifts of God, let us respond by
giving grateful praise to the Giver."

Counsels on Diets & Foods, 231

Breakfast Patties

1 ½ c. uncooked oatmeal	1 T. nutritional yeast flakes
1 c. wheat germ	⅛ tsp. sage
1 T. yeast	⅛ tsp. garlic powder
¼ c. water	1 med. onion, chopped fine
4 tsp. Bragg's liquid aminos (unfermented soy sauce)	¼ c. chopped walnuts
	1 ⅓ c. soy or nut milk
1 tsp. salt	½ c. tofu, mashed

In a small bowl dissolve yeast in ¼ cup warm water. In blender place tofu and soy milk. Blend until smooth. In a large bowl, place oatmeal, wheat germ, Bragg's liquid aminos, walnuts, garlic powder, nutritional yeast, salt, onion, and sage. Mix together well, then add tofu mixture and yeast mixture until mixed thoroughly. Make into patties. Fry in a small amount of oil, or bake in the oven on a cookie sheet for 15 minutes on each side. Serve plain or with favorite gravy.

Potato Cakes

3 c. mashed potatoes	¼ tsp. tumeric
½ lb. tofu	1 tsp. salt
2 T. parsley, dried	1 med. onion, chopped
1 ½ tsp. chicken style seasoning	

Saute onion in oil or water until tender. Blend tofu, parsley, chicken-style seasoning, and tumeric until smooth. Mix together mashed potatoes, onion, and tofu mixture. Shape into patties and brown in oil, about 4 minutes on each side.

Creole Frittata

1 pkg. Mori-nu tofu	1 med. onion, diced
3 T. lemon juice	½ c. green pepper, diced
1 tsp. basil	2 garlic cloves, minced
½ tsp. cilantro	1 c. cooked rice
1 tsp. salt	1 c. chopped tomatoes
½ tsp. cayenne pepper (optional)	Tofu cheese (optional)
1 T. oil or water	

In blender, place tofu, lemon juice, basil, cilantro, salt, and cayenne and blend until smooth. Saute onion, green pepper, and garlic in oil or water in a nonstick fry pan until tender. Then add rice and cook for an additional 3–4 minutes. Add tofu mixture and tomatoes and stir well. Place in an oiled or sprayed pie pan and bake at 350° for 30 minutes. If using the cheese, cover the top of the frittata and return to the oven until cheese melts.

Fruit Topping

½ c. frozen white grape/raspberry juice concentrate (100% juice)
2 T. cornstarch or arrowroot
1–12 oz. bag frozen fruit (strawberries, raspberries, or blueberries)
½ c. water

Dissolve the cornstarch (arrowroot) in cold water, then thicken with juice in a saucepan, over medium-low heat, stirring constantly. When thick add frozen fruit and simmer for 2 minutes. Turn off the heat. If using more fruit (14 oz or 16 oz bag), add 1 additional tablespoon of cornstarch. If using peaches, use ½ cup of frozen white grape/peach juice. You can also try it with ½ cup apple juice concentrate and add 3 cups sliced fresh apples, 1 teaspoon coriander, but you need to simmer for 10 minutes to soften the apples.

Quick and Easy Hash Browns

4 medium potatoes, shredded
Salt to taste

Wash and peel (optional) potatoes. Using a grater, shred potatoes. Place on pre-heated waffle iron. Cover and cook for 15–20 minutes until browned. Salt to taste and serve.

Wonderful Waffles

½ c. nuts (almonds/raw cashews)
1 tsp. salt
2 T. honey (optional)
3 c. water
3 c. oatmeal

In blender, process nuts with ½ c. of the water until smooth. Add salt, honey, water, and oatmeal. Blend until well mixed. Let stand 5 minutes. Preheat waffle iron, Spray with cooking spray. Pour batter into waffle iron and bake until lightly browned. Serve hot with your favorite jam, fruit sauce, or maple syrup. Makes 8–9 4-inch waffles.

Variation: Omit nuts and substitute 3 c. soy milk for the water.

Tip: Make a double batch and freeze the extras for popping in the toaster on a busy morning.

"Iron rusts from disuse, stagnant water loses its purity and in cold weather becomes frozen; even so does inaction sap the vigor of the mind."
—Leonardo da Vinci

Favorite Toast Toppings

Variation #1
Multi-grain Bread
Peanut Butter
Applesauce

Toast bread slices, spread with your favorite peanut (or other nut) butter. Next, top with some applesauce. Enjoy!

Variation #2 - Date-Nut Butter
1 c. walnuts or almonds
½ c. dates
1 c. water

Place all ingredients in blender and process until smooth. Chill and enjoy.

Fruit Sauce

1 ½ c. fruit juice
¼ c. tapioca
2 c. berries or chopped fruit

Cook juice and tapioca together over medium heat, until thickened. Add berries or chopped fruit. Serve over waffles, toast, or pancakes.

Rainy Day Crepes

1 ½ c. oatmeal
½ c. rye flour (optional-use other flour)
½ c. unbleached flour
½ c. raw cashews
2 T. oil
¼ c. honey
½ tsp. EnerG baking powder
½ tsp. salt
2 ½–2 ¾ c. water

Place all ingredients in blender and process until smooth. Pour ½ c. of batter on a preheated oil sprayed or non-stick griddle. Bake until top looks a bit dry around the edges. Turn crepe over and bake until lightly browned. Makes 8 large crepes. Serve warm with favorite fruit sauce or maple syrup.

French Toast

½ c. raw cashews
1 ¼ c. water
1 T. honey
2 T. cornstarch
½ tsp. vanilla
¼ tsp. coriander
¼ tsp. salt
8 slices bread

Place first 7 ingredients in blender and process until very smooth. Pour into a bowl. Dip bread slices in batter. Place on pre-heated, oil sprayed griddle, and cook until lightly browned. Brown on both sides. Serve warm with fruit sauce, maple syrup. or jam.

*"Blessed are those who give without remembering
and receive without forgetting."*

—Unknown

Hot Muesli

½ c.–¾ c. soy milk powder
3 c. water
2 ½ c. oatmeal
3 large apples, cored, and cubed

1 tsp. vanilla
1 c. dates or raisins
½ c. unsweetened shredded coconut
1 tsp. salt

Combine all the dry ingredients. Mix vanilla and water together. Pour the liquid mixture over the dry ingredients and mix well. Pour into an oil sprayed 9 x 13" pan. Cover with foil. Refrigerate overnight In the morning bake at 350° for 30 minutes, then uncover and bake for another 30 minutes. Serve with honey and milk.

Mixed Grain Cereal

1 ½ c. mixed grains
8 c. water
1 tsp. salt

Put grains, water and salt in the top part of a double boiler. Put several inches of water in the lower part of the double boiler. Steam for one hour or more stirring occasionally. Turn off the heat. Cover and let steam until serving time. Use any variety of mixed grains such as: millet, oats, flaked rye, rice, cracked barley, wheat, and buckwheat.

Tip: Soak grains 24 hours instead of cooking. Great for travel when cooking is not available. Place water and grains in ziplock bag for soaking.

Great Granola

4 ½ c. oatmeal
¾ c. chopped nuts
¾ c. coconut, shredded
½ c. wheatgerm
½ c. cornmeal
1 c. dried fruit (chopped; raisins, cherries, cranberries, pineapple, etc.

¼ c. honey
½ tsp. salt
¾ c. fruit juice (apple, white grape, pineapple; use a bit more if neccesary, to moisten)

Combine all ingredients except dried fruit and mix until evenly moistened. Pour onto baking sheets and bake at 250° for approx. 1 hour, stirring every 15 minutes until lightly browned, dry, and crispy. Stir in the dried fruit during the last 15-minute bake. Cool and store in an airtight container.

Scrambled Tofu

1 lb. water-packed tofu, firm or extra-firm
1 T. chicken style seasoning
½ tsp. garlic powder
½ tsp. salt
2 tsp. onion powder
¼ tsp turmeric (for color)
2 tsp. oil (optional, may use water)
½ c. chopped pimento or red pepper
½ c. chopped green pepper
½ c. chopped green onions

Saute green onion, pimentos, and peppers in oil or water in a large frying pan. Mash tofu and mix in seasonings, then add to the frying pan and heat for about 10 minutes.

Hearty Breakfast Burritos

1 T. extra virgin olive oil
1 med. potato, shredded
1 sm. onion, chopped
½ green pepper, chopped
½ red bell pepper, chopped
1 T. Braggs liquid aminos, optional
½ tsp. cumin
½ tsp. ground coriander
salt to taste
1 lb. Firm or extra-firm tofu, crumbled
½ c. mushrooms, sliced
¼ c. cilantro, chopped
8 whole wheat tortillas, warmed
salsa, warmed

Heat oil in a skillet over medium heat. Add onions and potatoes and sauté for several minutes. Add peppers, and seasonings until vegetables are tender. Then add tofu, mushrooms, and cilantro. Stir together and continue cooking until warmed throughout Remove from heat. Place approximately ⅓ cup of mixture on each tortilla. Roll up and top with salsa.

"Be the living expression of God's kindness:
kindness in your face, kindness in your eyes, kindness in your smile.
Let no one ever come to you without leaving better and happier."

—Mother Teresa

Breads & Spreads

"I am the living bread which came down from heaven.
If anyone eats of this bread, he will live forever;
and the bread that I shall give is my flesh,
which I shall give for the life of the world."

John 6:51 NKJV

Squash Bread with Flaxseed

3 c. warm water
¼ c. soy milk powder
2 c. cooked squash (or pumpkin)
½ ground flaxseed
3 T. olive oil
⅓ c. honey
1 T. salt
2 T. yeast
4 c. whole wheat flour
7 c. unbleached flour (approximately)

Mix all ingredients except flour together in a large bowl. Stir in the whole wheat flour. Gradually work the unbleached flour into the mixture, kneading continuously for about 10 minutes. Cover the dough with a towel, and allow to rise until double in size. Punch down and shape into loaves (4 medium or 3 large loaves). Place in greased or sprayed pans & allow to rise once more until doubled. Bake at 400° for 10 minutes then reduce heat to 350° until done—approximately 35–40 minutes <u>total time</u>. Thanks to Sharon Inman for this recipe.

Rye Bread

3 ¾ c. boiling water
⅓ c. honey
1 ½ c. rolled rye
1 T. salt
3 c. rye flour
2 T. caraway seeds (optional)
⅓ c. molasses
⅓ c. oil (or applesauce)
2 T. yeast
1 ½ c. whole wheat flour
2 ½–4 c. unbleached flour

Pour water over rolled rye, then add honey, molasses, and oil (applesauce), let cool down. When mixture is just warm, stir in yeast, then add salt, whole wheat flour and rye flour. Add remaining flour to make a moderately stiff dough. Knead until smooth and satiny, 10–15 minutes. Shape dough into a ball and place in a lightly greased bowl. Cover and let rise until double. Punch down and divide into 3 portions. Shape into loaves, place in greased pans, and let rise until double. Bake at 350° for about 35 minutes.

Basic Whole Wheat Muffin Mix

2 c. warm water
2 T. honey
1 ½ T. dry yeast
2 T. oil
1 ½ tsp. salt
3 c. whole wheat flour
½ c. white flour

Combine the first three ingredients and let stand about 5–8 min., until yeast bubbles. Then stir in remaining ingredients. Oil muffin tins. Fill ⅔ full with batter. Or drop by large spoonfuls onto oiled cookie sheet. Let raise 10 min. Bake at 350° for 30–35 min. Makes 12–18. Or place in oiled 8 x 8 pan, let rise 15 min. Bake at 350° for 40–45 min.

Muffin Variations: Use the Basic Whole Wheat Muffin Mix just as it is, along with any of these variations (additions). When recipe reads to leave out certain items, this pertains to the Basic Mix ingredients.

Soy, Millet or Buckwheat
½ c. soy, millet, or buckwheat flour (omit the white flour in basic recipe).

Raisin Orange
¾ c. raisins and 1 T. dried orange peel

Date Bran
½ c. oat or wheat bran and ⅔ c. dates

Blueberry
1 ½ c. berries
1 tsp. vanilla
¼ c. sweetener
(omit ½ c. water in basic recipe)

Recipe used with permission from JoAnn Rachor, (1950). *Of These Ye May Freely Eat*. Sunfield, MI: Family Health Publications, 11–13.

Eden's Bounty

Pineapple
1-20 oz. can crushed pineapple (well drained)
2 T. sweetener
1 tsp. vanilla
(omit ½ c. water in basic recipe)

Banana Nut
2 c. mashed banana and ½ c. chopped nuts or seeds
(omit ⅔ c. water in basic recipe)

Jam
¾ c. dried fruit jam
After filling muffin tin drop ¾–1 tsp. of jam on top of batter then let rise 10 min.

Cornbread
1 ¾ c. cornmeal
¾ c. white flour
1 T. oil
(omit ½ c. water and 2 ½ c. whole wheat flour in the basic recipe)

Barley, Rice, or Oat
1 c. barley, rice or oat flour
(omit white flour and ½ c. of whole wheat flour in the basic recipe)

Cheese
2 c. cheese sauce
(omit ⅔ c. water in the basic recipe)

Caraway Rye
1 c. rye flour
2 T. Molasses
1 ½ tsp. caraway seed
(omit ½ c. of whole wheat flour, ½ c. white flour, and honey in the basic recipe)

Cranberry, Carrot, Zucchini or Apple
½ c. honey
½ c. chopped nuts or seeds
1 ½ tsp. coriander
1 ½ tsp. dried orange peel
1 ½ c. cranberry (briefly blended) or 2 c. of grated carrot, zucchini or apple
2 tsp. vanilla

(Omit ½–¾ c. of the water depending on which fruit or vegetable is being used. Leave out ½ c. water for the cranberry and carrot and ¾ c. water for the apple and zucchini muffins.

Tahini
⅓ c. Tahini
(omit ¼ c. water from the basic recipe)

Oatmeal Wheat Germ Bread

2 qts. hot water (8 c.)	4 T. yeast
¾ c. honey	Whole wheat flour
2 T. salt	4 c. oatmeal
½ c. oil	2 c. wheat germ
¼ c. molasses	White flour

Mix together hot water, honey, oil, salt and add enough whole wheat flour to make a thin mush consistency. Then add the oatmeal, dry yeast, and wheat germ, and mix well. Continue to add whole wheat and/or white flour as needed until dough is no longer sticky. Knead 15 minutes adding flour to keep dough from sticking. Place in a large bowl, cover and rise until double in size. Punch down and let rise a second time. After second rising, punch down dough and form into loaves. Raise until double in size. Makes 8 loaves. Bake at 350° for 1 hour.

"There is no right way to do a wrong thing."
—Unknown

Whole Wheat Bread

½ c. warm water
2 T. yeast
1 T. honey
2 ½ c. warm water
1 T. salt

½ c. honey
½ c. olive oil
2 c. unbleached flour
6 c. whole wheat flour

Mix together warm water, yeast and 1 T. honey in a small bowl and let stand. In a large bowl, mix all of the other ingredients with the exception of the whole wheat flour. Cool mixture to lukewarm and stir in yeast mixture. Mix well, knead for 10 minutes until smooth and satiny. Let dough rise until double in size, about 1–1 ½ hours. Form into loaves, place in pans and let dough rise again until double. Bake at 350° for 30 minutes. Makes 3 medium or 2 large loaves.

Holiday Rolls

2 ½ c. warm water
¾ c. honey
2 pkgs. of yeast
⅓ c. olive oil
1 c. mashed potatoes
3 ½ tsps. salt
1 c. oatmeal
1 c. whole wheat flour
4–4 ½ c. unbleached flour

Dissolve yeast in warm water with honey. After yeast bubbles add oil, salt, and potatoes and mix well. Next add oatmeal, whole wheat flour, and mix until well blended. Add 2 cups of unbleached flour and continue to add remaining flour ½ to 1 cup at a time until dough is no longer sticky to touch. Knead dough for 10 minutes. Cover and let rise in a warm place until double in size. Punch down, knead lightly, and shape into rolls. Place rolls on a greased pan ½ inch apart. Let rolls rise until double in size. Bake at 400° until golden brown. Thanks to Sharon Inman for sharing this recipe.

Pizza Dough

3 c. whole wheat pastry flour
1 c. lukewarm water
1 T. yeast
½ tsp. salt

Dissolve yeast in water and let it stand about 5 minutes. Add flour to the yeast mixture. Knead and blend well. Let dough rise until double in size, punch down and let rise again. Roll out and place on a pizza stone or oil-sprayed pan. Bake at 400° until light brown. If using a regular pan and not a stone, check the bottom of the pizza often. Add your favorite tomato sauce, toppings and cheese.

Tip: When making pizza, pour the sauce in your blender. Add a carrot or two, fresh sweet pepper, broccoli, or other veggies your family doesn't get enough of. Blend until smooth.

Brown Rice Bread

2 c. warm water or soy milk
¼ c. oil
¼ c. honey
2 tsp. salt
2 c. cooked brown rice
1 pkg yeast
2 c. whole wheat flour
¼ –⅓ c. wheat germ
¼ c. ground flax seed

Mix together water, oil, honey, salt, rice, yeast, wheat germ, flax seed, and flour. Knead 10 minutes, add extra flour if needed, knead until smooth and elastic. Let dough rise, punch down, shape into loaves, let rise again in pans. Bake at 400° about 30 minutes. Thanks to Sharon Inman for this recipe.

Multi-Grain Bread

2 pkgs. yeast (2 Tbs.)
¼ c. warm water
1 tsp. honey
3 ½ c. warm water
½ c. honey
1 T. salt
½ c. olive oil
½ c. flax seed, ground

1 c. oatmeal
4 ½ c. whole wheat flour
   (more or less as needed)
2 c. white unbleached flour
½ c. wheat germ
½ c. corn meal
½ c. millet flour

Soften yeast in ½ cup warm water, with 1 tsp. honey in a small bowl and let stand. In a large bowl combine the rest of the ingredients with the exception of the unbleached and whole wheat flour. Cool mixture to lukewarm and stir in yeast. Add flour and stir to make moderately stiff dough. Turn out on a lightly floured surface. Knead the dough until smooth and satiny. Shape dough into a ball. Place in a lightly greased bowl. Cover and let rise in a warm place until double. Punch down. Divide into 3 portions. Shape into loaves and place in pans. Let dough rise until double (about 1 hour). Bake about 35 minutes at 350°.

Tip: Substitute an equal amount of applesauce for the oil in any bread recipe.

No Oil Whole Wheat Bread

6 c. whole wheat flour
2 c. oatmeal
4 T. dry yeast

c. honey
1 T. salt
5 c. hot tap water

In a large bowl combine hot tap water, salt, honey, and 6 cups of whole wheat flour. Mix well, then add yeast and oatmeal and mix thoroughly. Continue adding whole wheat flour until dough starts to pull from the edge of the bowl. (You can use an electric mixer. If you do, mix on low for 10 minutes). If you are making it by hand, knead for 10 minutes. Shape dough into loaves and place in sprayed pans, or pans that have been sprinkled with cornmeal. Let loaves rise until double, bake at 350° for 45 minutes to 1 hour.

*"Morning exercise, walking in the free, invigorating air of heaven…
is the surest safeguard against colds, coughs, congestion of the brain and lungs…
and an hundred other diseases."*

—E. G. White, *Healthful Living* (1898).

SPREADS

Pecan Spread

1 lb. tofu, drained
1 c. pecan meal
½ c. celery, chopped
½ –¾ c. non-dairy mayonnaise
⅔ c. chopped black olives
1 tsp. onion powder
1 tsp. garlic powder
½ tsp. salt

Mash tofu with a fork, add the remaining ingredients and mix well. Best if refrigerated for at least 3 hours before serving.

Garbanzo Spread

1-15 oz can garbanzos, drained
½ c. chopped celery
¼ c. chopped green onion
2 T. chopped pimento
½ c. non-dairy mayonnaise (more or less)
Dash garlic powder
1 tsp. chicken style seasoning (optional)

Mash garbanzos, add mayonnaise, seasonings, stir in onions, pimentos, and celery. Refrigerate. Serve with crackers or in sandwiches.

Eggless Salad

1 lb. firm tofu, drained
1 T. chicken-style seasoning (see "This & That")
½ c. pickle relish
½ c. diced onions
Non-dairy mayonnaise

Mash tofu until medium fine. Blend in chicken-style seasoning. Stir in pickles and onions. Add favorite non-dairy mayonnaise to desired consistency.

Soups

"Though no one can go back and make a brand new start my friend, anyone can start from now and make a brand new end."

—Unknown

Barley Soup

8 c. water
1 c. med. pearl barley
4 potatoes, cubed
1 large onion, diced
2 large carrots, diced
1 ½ tsp. salt
1–2 bay leaves

Cook barley in water for 15 minutes. Add vegetables and seasonings. Simmer until tender.

Vegetable Soup

8 c. water
3 medium potatoes, cubed
2 c. chopped cabbage
2 onions, diced
1 c. chopped celery
2 c. frozen mixed vegetables
1 ½ tsp. salt
1 tsp. basil
1 T. garlic salt
1 T. onion powder
2 T. basil
1 c. elbow macaroni, uncooked (optional)
3 c. tomatoes, diced

Put water in large pan. Place the remaining ingredients (except macaroni and tomatoes) in pan and bring to a boil. Add tomatoes and simmer until nearly done. Add macaroni and continue to simmer until tender. Thin with water if needed.

Vegetable Soup II

½ c. uncooked brown rice
5 c. water
3 medium potatoes
1 large carrot
1 ½ c. chopped celery
1 ½ tsp salt
1 lb. bag frozen mixed vegetables
1–15 oz. can tomato sauce
1 tsp. basil
¼ tsp. garlic powder

Place water and rice in a large pan and begin cooking while you prepare other ingredients. Add potatoes, carrots, and celery to the simmering rice pan and cook for 20 minutes. Add the remainder of ingredients and simmer until vegetables and rice are tender.

Lentil and Bell Pepper Chili

1 teaspoon olive oil
1 large onion, chopped
1 large green pepper, chopped
1 large red pepper, chopped
1 large yellow pepper, chopped
4 garlic cloves, minced

1 teaspoon chili powder
2 teaspoons ground cumin
2-14 ½ ounce cans diced tomatoes with green chili peppers
5 ½ c. chicken style broth
2 c. dry lentils

Optional topping:
½ c. chopped cilantro
1 teaspoon grated lime zest (may use lime juice)
½ c. onion, chopped

Sauté onions and peppers in oil until soft. Add garlic, cumin, and chili powder. Stir well, add tomatoes. Add chicken style broth. (Use 1 teaspoon of chicken style seasoning per each cup of water). Add lentils and cook on a medium heat until lentils are tender, about 25 minutes. Stir the cilantro, lime zest, and onion together, and sprinkle each serving of chili with a bit of this mixture. May add a dollop of sour cream substitute (see This & That). Thanks to Chris Huge for sharing this recipe.

Minestrone Soup

1 c. red beans, cooked
1 c. kidney beans, cooked
1 c. northern white beans, cooked
1 c. lima beans, cooked
1 c. garbanzo beans, cooked
1 c. pinto beans, cooked
1 large onion, chopped
2 cloves garlic, minced

1 ½ c. celery, chopped
1/2 c. fresh parsley
1 ½ qt. tomatoes
2 c. cabbage, shredded
4 c. zucchini squash, cubed or sliced
2 ½ tsp. salt
1 tsp. oregano
1 tsp. basil

Saute onion, garlic, parsley, and celery in a small amount of water or oil until tender. In a large cooking pan, place beans and sauteed vegetables, tomatoes, and seasonings. Simmer covered for about 45 minutes. Add cabbage, squash and enough water to cover all ingredients. Continue cooking until cabbage and squash are tender. Serve hot. This is a good soup to freeze and use at a later date.

Tip: Some of these soup recipes make a rather large quantity. Cut the recipe in half or share with a friend or neighbor.

Potato Broccoli Soup

10 medium potatoes, peeled and diced
3 T. chicken style seasoning
1 T. onion powder
1 tsp. garlic powder
Salt to taste
9 c. water
1 onion, diced
1 ¾ c. raw cashews
1 c. cooked rice
4 c. small broccoli flowerets
½ c. chopped mushrooms (optional)
3 tsp. salt or to taste

Place first 6 ingredients in a large pan on the stove. In a blender, blend cashews, cooked rice, onion, and enough water from the pan to blend until a smooth consistency. Pour mixture into the pan with the potatoes. Cook until potatoes are soft and done. Last, add the broccoli flowerets and cook for about 5 additional minutes. Ready to serve. For a festive look, garnish with a sprig of fresh parsley.

Chunky Potato Soup

1 large onion
2 stalks celery
3 medium carrots
10–12 medium potatoes
3 qt. water + 1 T. salt
¾ c. raw cashews
⅓ c. unbleached flour
2–3 T. nutritional yeast
1 T. parsley (dried)

Put vegetables, water, and salt in a large pot. Bring to boil, lower the heat and simmer for 30 minutes or until tender. While vegetables are cooking, place cashews and 1 cup of hot water from the cooking pot in the blender. Blend until very smooth. Add flour and nutritional yeast. If too thick, add a bit more water from the pot. When the vegetables are done stir in the cashew mixture, continuing to stire until well mixed. Return to boil. Remove from heat. Add parsley and serve.

Variation: Add 1 cup cooked rice or barley.

Lentil Soup

2 qts. water
1 lb. baby carrots, whole or chopped
1 large onion, chopped
1 T. parsley, dried
1 lb. lentils (uncooked)
1 large stalk celery, chopped
½ tsp. basil (optional)
Salt to taste

Place all ingredients in a large pot and cook until tender.

Tomato Soup

2 c. water
¾ c. raw cashews
2 T. nutritional yeast
2 T. honey
1 qt. tomatoes (4 c.)
1-8 oz. can tomato sauce

1 medium onion
½ c. sliced olives
½ tsp. oregano
1 tsp. basil
1 tsp. salt
1 c. fresh tomatoes, diced (optional)

In a blender, puree cashews, water, nutritional yeast, and honey until smooth. Place contents into a large pan. Then place canned tomatoes, tomato sauce, onion, olives, oregano, basil, and salt in the blender and whiz until smooth. Add this to the cashew mixture. Cook on medium heat until hot. Add fresh tomatoes if desired. Cook another 5 minutes.

Vegetarian "Chicken" Noodle Soup

2 Tbs. light olive oil
1 med. onion, thinly sliced
1–2 stalks celery, thinly sliced
1 bay leaf
2 sm. carrots, sliced in rounds or diced
1 c. shredded Worthington frozen "Chic-ketts"*
8 c. water
2 Tbs. nutritional yeast

½ tsp. garlic powder
1 ½ tsp. onion powder
2 tsp. salt or salt to taste
⅛ tsp. poultry seasoning or a pinch each of ground marjoram, sage, thyme, and rosemary
2 c. dried wide noodles
1 c. frozen peas
1 tsp. dried parsley

In a 2-quart pot, sauté onions and celery in the oil until golden. Next add the bay leaf, cut carrots, shredded "Chic-ketts" and water. Season with nutritional yeast, garlic powder, salt and herbs. Bring to a boil and add the two cups of dried noodle. Reduce to a simmer. Skim off foam with a spoon. When noodles are tender, add the peas and parsley. Return to a simmer for several minutes. Remove from heat and serve.

* Vegetable protein found in the frozen section at most health food stores or use other chicken substitute.

A big thank-you to Beverly Kinsley for sharing this recipe.

Salads & Vegetables

"I believe in the sun even when it is not shining.
I believe in love even when not feeling it.
I believe in God even when He is silent."

—Unknown

SALADS

Mediterranean Salad

4 c. chickpeas (garbanzos)
1 c. green olives with pimentos
1 c. chopped parsley (fresh)
1 c. green onions, chopped

½ c. celery, chopped
2 c. diced tomatoes
4 tsp. onion powder
1 tsp. garlic powder

Mix all together. Chill and serve.

Raw Cranberry Relish

1 orange, peeled and quartered
2 apples, cored and quartered
1–16 oz. bag fresh cranberries
½ c. pecans, chopped
⅓–½ c. honey

Chop orange, apples, and cranberries in a food processor or blender until desired consistency. Place in a mixing bowl. Add pecans and honey, mix well. Chill in refrigerator for several hours or overnight to blend flavors. Thanks to Marilyn Anderson for this recipe.

Cucumber Dill Salad

4 med. cucumbers
2 tsp. salt
ice cubes
1 sm. onion, chopped fine

1 ½ tsp. dill weed
1 recipe tofu sour cream (see "This and That")

Peel and slice cucumbers, place in a 13 x 9 inch casserole dish, then sprinkle with salt and add ice cubes on the top. Place in the refrigerator for about 15 minutes, then rinse and drain cucumbers. Press out the excess water. Add onion, dill weed and tofu sour cream. Mix well. Tastes best when chilled for at least 2 hours.

Salads & Vegetables

Zucchini Slaw

2 yellow summer squash
2 zucchini squash
1 onion, chopped

2 sweet peppers (green, red, or yellow) chopped
Slaw dressing (See This & That)

Grate zucchini and summer squash. Mix in other vegetables. Mix in slaw dressing. Thanks to Chris Huge for this recipe.

Grandma's Potato Salad

6 c. cubed cooked potatoes
1 onion, chopped
1 c. celery, chopped
1 c. green pepper, chopped
½ c. carrots, chopped

1 tsp. salt
½–1 c. non-dairy mayonnaise
1 c. tofu
1/8 tsp. tumeric
1 T. chicken style-seasoning

In a small fry pan, coated with oil spray, combine tofu (mash), tumeric, and chicken-style seasoning. Stir and cook until it has a scrambled egg look, about 5 minutes. Remove from heat and cool. Mix together potatoes, vegetables, tofu mixture, seasonings, and non-dairy mayonnaise. Chill before serving. For a festive look, mold in a dish and chill for several hours before serving. Garnish with fresh parsley, cherry or grape tomatoes.

Hot or Cold Pasta Salad

1 lb. whole wheat rotini, cooked
1 8-oz. can mushroom pieces, drained
½ c. black olives, sliced
½ c. bell pepper, chopped
¼ c. green onion, chopped

1 large tomato, chopped
2 T. nutritional yeast
1 T. dried parsley
Salt to taste
Non-dairy mayonnaise

Cook rotini as per package directions. Combine all ingredients in a large mixing bowl, adding enough mayonnaise to moisten. Serve hot or cold.

Southwestern Salad

½ c. elbow macaroni or any small pasta
⅓ c. olive oil
⅓ c. lime juice
1 T. cumin
½ tsp. salt
1 tsp. garlic powder
1 T. cilantro

1 ½ c. corn (fresh, frozen, or canned)
2 c. black beans, cooked
2 c. tomatoes, chopped
1 small onion, chopped fine
½ green bell pepper, chopped
½ red bell pepper, chopped
⅔ c. black olives
⅔ c. salsa (mild, medium, or hot)

Cook pasta according to the package directions. Rinse and drain well. While pasta is cooking, place oil, lime juice, cilantro, cumin, salt, and garlic powder in the blender, and process until smooth. Place corn, black beans, tomatoes, olives, peppers, onion, and salsa in a large bowl. Mix well and slowly add dressing. Next add pasta and toss gently. Chill.

Vegetable Barley Salad

1 c. med. pearl barley
1 ½ c. chopped fresh mushrooms
1 c. chopped celery
1 c. chopped water chestnuts
1 c. chopped green pepper
½ c. shredded carrot
½ c. chopped green onions
2 garlic cloves, minced
1 T. dill weed

Dressing
1 tsp. dried basil
1 tsp. salt
1 tsp garlic powder
1 tsp. onion powder
½–⅔ c. Italian dressing

2 pkgs. George Washington Golden Broth or 2 T. veg. broth pwd.
3 c. water

In a sauce pan, mix water and broth, bring to a boil; stir in barley. Reduce heat, cover and simmer until tender, about 45 minutes. Mix together the remainder of the ingredients, except the dressing. After the barley is cooked, add to the above mixture. Mix well. Add the dressing next and stir to coat. Chill before serving.

Curried Pasta Salad

1 lb. uncooked pasta
1 c. tofu
1 c. frozen peas
1 sm. onion, chopped fine
1 T. curry or curry substitute

1/2 c. chopped pimentos
1 tsp. onion powder
1–1 ½ tsp. salt
⅛ tsp. tumeric
½ c. non-dairy mayonnaise

Cook pasta according to directions, rinse well with cold water and drain. While pasta is cooking, combine curry, onion powder, tumeric and tofu (mash with fork until it has a scrambled egg look) in an oil-sprayed frypan. Cook for 5 minutes, while stirring. Cook peas according to package directions. Combine pasta, salt, tofu, chopped onion, peas and pimentos with non-dairy mayonnaise. Mix well, and refrigerate before serving.

Mexican Taco Salad

1 lg. onion, chopped
4 med. tomatoes, chopped
¼ tsp. salt
1 head iceberg lettuce
1 can kidney beans, drained
1 c. bulgur wheat

1 ½ c. boiling water
7–8 oz. baked tortilla chips
½ c. chopped black olives
½ c.–¾ c. salsa
Avocado slices (optional)

Place bulgur wheat in a medium size bowl and pour boiling water over it. Cover and let stand at least 30 minutes. In a large fry pan, saute bulgur wheat in a small amount of oil or water, and add kidney beans, and salt. Simmer 10 minutes. In a large bowl, place onion, tomatoes, olives, and chopped lettuce, toss with salsa. Add bulgur wheat and beans to lettuce combination. Just before serving crush chips and toss into salad. Decorate with avocado slices if desired.

Favorite Macaroni Salad

1 lb. uncooked macaroni
1 onion, chopped
1 c. celery, chopped
1 c. sweet bell pepper, chopped (green, red, or yellow)
½ c. carrots, chopped
1 tsp. salt
½–1 c. non-dairy mayonnaise

Cook macaroni according to directions. Rinse, drain, and cool. Mix together macaroni, vegetables, salt, and non-dairy mayonnaise. Chill before serving.

Lentil Salad

1 lb. lentils, uncooked
6 c. water
3 cloves garlic, peeled
3 bay leaves
2 c. thinly sliced green onions, including tops
1 can green chili peppers
½ c. oil
5 T. lemon juice
1 tsp. grated lime peel
4 large garlic cloves, minced
1 T. cumin
1 ½ tsp. cilantro
1 c. fresh chopped tomatoes
Salt to taste

Rinse lentils and place them in a large pan with the water, 3 whole cloves of garlic, and bay leaves. Bring to a boil over high heat. Cover, reduce heat and simmer until lentils are tender (about 25–30 minutes). Drain well, rinse with cold water and discard bay leaves. Cool for about 20 minutes. Meanwhile, in a container with a tight fitting lid, combine the oil, lime peel, lemon juice, minced garlic, cumin, and cilantro. Cover and shake well. Pour over the lentils, add the green onions, green chilies, and tomatoes. Stir mixture lightly. Add salt to taste. Cover and let stand at room temperature for at least 30 minutes (for flavors to absorb) then refrigerate until ready to serve.

Raspberry Salad

2 ½ lbs. raspberries
16 oz. crushed pineapple, undrained
10 oz. mandarin oranges
4 med. bananas, sliced
Milled cane sugar to taste

Mix raspberries, oranges, and pineapple together. Add milled cane sugar to taste, if desired. Best if refrigerated overnight. Slice bananas and stir in just before serving. Many thanks to Sue Wade for this recipe.

VEGETABLES

Scalloped Potatoes

8 medium potatoes, sliced
1 med. onion, diced
1 c. raw cashews
3 T. cornstarch or arrowroot powder
2 tsp. onion powder
2 tsp. salt
4 c. water

In a blender, place 2 cups of the water, seasonings, arrowroot, and cashews, blend until smooth. While blending gradually add remaining water, until smooth. Slice potatoes and put half of them in an oiled sprayed casserole pan. Place ½ of diced onion on top of potatoes. Pour 2 cups of cashew mixture on top of potatoes and onions. Repeat layers with remaining potatoes, onions, and cashew mixture. Cover with foil. Bake at 350° for 45 minutes, then bake uncovered for 15 minutes, or until browned.

Squash Casserole

1 lb. yellow summer squash
1 lg. onion, chopped
1 stalk celery, chopped
1 lg. green pepper, chopped
3 T. rice, uncooked
1-16-oz. can tomatoes
Salt to taste
Thyme to taste

Mix all ingredients together, then place in an oil-sprayed casserole dish. Bake 1 ½ hours at 350°.

Baked Potatoes

Potatoes, washed and scrubbed. One per person. Cover with foil and bake at 350° for 1 hour. For extra special potatoes, try one of the following toppings.

Creamed Curried Vegetables

4 c. water
¼ c. Bragg's liquid aminos
1 ½ c. raw cashews
4 T. cornstarch or arrowroot powder
1 small can sliced mushrooms

1 ½ tsp. onion powder
1 tsp. garlic powder
1 tsp. curry or coriander
1 tsp. salt
4 c. mixed vegetables (fresh or frozen)

Blend the first 4 ingredients until smooth. Then place in a saucepan on the stove. Add mushrooms and seasonings, stir until thickened. If using fresh vegetables, cook until tender then add to the hot gravy. If using frozen vegetables, thaw them by running cold water over them, drain, and then add to the gravy. Also, delicious served over baked potatoes, rice, couscous, or pasta.

Black Bean Topping

4 c. black beans, cooked
1 can diced tomatoes with green chilies

1 ½ tsp. onion powder
1 ½ tsp. garlic powder
2 tsp. cumin

Mix all together and heat in a sauce pan, crock pot or microwave. Serve over potatoes, couscous, or rice.

"Tact is the art of making guests feel at home when you wish that's where they were."

Spinach Patties

¼ c. ground flax seed
⅔ c. boiling water
½ medium green pepper, chopped
1 large onion, chopped
2 celery stalks, chopped
1 ½ c. grated carrots

1 10-oz. package chopped frozen spinach, thawed
⅓ c. whole wheat flour
1 ¼ tsp. salt
¼ c. nutritional yeast flakes
1 box Mori-Nu, silken tofu (firm), mashed

Combine flax seed and water in a small bowl and let stand. Next, steam pepper, onion, and celery in a small amount of water until tender. Remove from heat. In a large bowl, mix together carrots, spinach, flour, yeast flakes, and salt. Combine the sauteed mixture, tofu, and the flax seed mixture. Lightly oil a heavy skillet and heat to medium-hot. Drop mixture by large tablespoonfuls into skillet. Flatten patties slightly with the back of a spoon. Cook until lightly browned, turn and brown on other side. Serve warm as is or with your favorite non-dairy sour cream.

Maple Glazed Sweet Potatoes

1 c. apple juice or cider (divided)
4 tsp. cornstarch
½ c. maple syrup
1 tsp. coriander
½ tsp. salt
2 lbs. sweet potatoes (about 3 large), cut into ¾" cubes (5 cups)
2 T. chopped pecans

In a small bowl, combine 2 tablespoons of the apple juice and the cornstarch; mix well. Set aside. In a large nonstick skillet, combine remaining apple juice, syrup, coriander, and salt; mix well. Bring to a boil. Add potatoes; stir to coat well. Return to a boil. Reduce heat; cover and simmer 8–10 minutes or just until potatoes are tender. Stir cornstarch mixture into potato mixture; cook and stir over medium-high heat until bubbly and thickened. Serve sprinkled with pecans.

Tip: In a hurry? Use canned, drained sweet potatoes. Simmer first 5 ingredients uncovered for about five minutes. Add sweet potatoes and simmer just until warmed. Sprinkle on pecans and serve.

Creole Soybeans

4 c. green soybeans, cooked
½ c. chopped onion
1 green pepper, chopped
1 c. tomato paste
1 tsp. garlic powder
½ tsp. onion powder
1 bay leaf crushed
1 ½ c. water

Saute onion, green pepper, and bay leaf in a small amount of oil or water until tender. Add tomato paste and water, blend well. Next add garlic powder, onion powder, and green soybeans. Simmer 15 minutes. Ready to serve.

"Life is like a grindstone...whether it grinds you down or polishes you up depends on the stuff you are made of."
—Unknown

Main Dishes

"Behold, I have given you every herb bearing seed which is upon the face of all the earth, and every tree, in the which is the fruit of a tree yielding seed; to you it shall be for meat."

Genesis 1:29, KJV

Jambalaya

1 T. oil or water	1 tsp. Italian seasoning
1 c. chopped onion	¼ tsp. cayenne pepper
1 c. chopped green pepper	1 tsp. onion powder
3 garlic cloves, minced	⅛ tsp. fennel seed, crushed
2 c. water	1 c. uncooked rice
2 c. chopped tomatoes	1 can red beans, drained
1-8 oz. can tomato sauce	1 can kidney beans, drained

In a large skillet heat 1 T. oil or 1 T. water until hot. Add green pepper, garlic, and onion. Cook and stir until tender. Stir in 2 cups of water, tomatoes, tomato sauce, Italian seasoning, cayenne, and fennel seed. Bring to a boil. Add rice and stir. Reduce heat to low, cover and cook until rice is tender, stirring occasionally. Stir in beans. Cover and cook additional 10 minutes.

Easy Mexican Black Beans and Rice

2 16-oz. can black beans (4 c. cooked black beans with liquid)	1 T. cumin
1 16-oz. can chopped tomatoes with green chilies	1 tsp. cilantro
1-2 fresh tomatoes, chopped	1 tsp. garlic powder
½-1 c. green onions, chopped	1 tsp. onion powder
½-⅔ c. sliced black olives	4-5 c. cooked brown rice
	1 recipe of soy sour cream (see This and That)

Place cooked rice in a casserole dish. Combine beans and seasonings and pour over rice. Top with canned tomatoes and green chilies. Cover with foil and bake for 35–45 minutes at 350°. While baking make sour cream recipe. Remove beans from the oven, spread sour cream on top of beans, then place olives, tomatoes, green onions, on top of sour cream.

Main Dishes

Asparagus Tofu Stir-Fry

1–2 pounds fresh asparagus
1 lb. water packed tofu (well drained)
1–2 garlic cloves, minced
1 T. oil or water
3–4 green onions, chopped
Salt to taste
Rice

Clean asparagus, break or cut into one inch pieces. Cube or break tofu into 1 inch pieces. Heat oil or water in skillet. Place all ingredients in skillet, cook on medium high heat and stir frequently. For extra flavor, add a dash of crushed red pepper. Thanks to Freida Perkins for this recipe.

Sweet Potato Veggie Stir-Fry

1 medium sweet potato, quartered & thinly sliced
1 small green pepper, cut in thin strips
4 green onions, chopped
2 carrots, thinly sliced
1 zucchini, thinly sliced
2 c. cooked brown rice
1 c. fresh mushrooms, sliced
¼ c. honey
¼ c. Bragg's liquid aminos (non-fermented soy sauce)
1 lb. tofu, water-packed, drained and cubed

Heat oil or water in a large heavy skillet. Stir fry green onions, sweet potato, green pepper, carrots, and zucchini until barely tender. Add rice, mushrooms, and tofu. Cook quickly until heated thoroughly. If necessary add more oil. Combine honey and Bragg's liquid aminos. Pour over mixture and stir. Serve immediately. Adapted from a recipe by Sharon Inman.

Veggie Stir-Fry

1 c. snow peas
2 c. sliced zucchini
2 cloves garlic, minced
2 T. arrowroot powder or cornstarch
½ tsp. ginger
1 c. orange juice
¼ c. Bragg's liquid aminos (non-fermented soy sauce)
2 T. oil or water
Hot cooked rice

In a small bowl combine the arrowroot and ginger, stir in orange juice, liquid aminos, and garlic. In wok or large skillet, place all veggies and stir-fry in oil or water until crisp. Pour sauce over the veggies and cook until slightly thickened. Serve over hot cooked rice.

Walnut Dressing

2 c. bread crumbs
1 medium onion chopped fine
½ c. celery chopped fine
½ c. chopped walnuts

1 T. chicken style seasoning
½ tsp. sage
¼ c. soy milk

Mix bread crumbs, walnuts, and seasonings together. Saute celery and onions in a small amount of water or oil. Mix all ingredients together. Place in a greased or oil-sprayed pan. Cover and bake at 350° for 30 minutes.

Speedy Sloppy Joes

2 c. TVP Beef-like
  (dehydrated, textured soy protein)
4 c. warm water

1 large onion, chopped
tofu
ketchup

Reconstitute TVP in water. While TVP is soaking, sauté onion in a bit of olive oil until transparent. Drain excess water from TVP and add TVP to onion. Add enough ketchup to make sloppy joe consistency. Serve over favorite bread or buns.

Almond Tofu Stir-Fry

2 T. oil or water
2 c. frozen tofu, thawed and broken
  into small pieces
2 garlic cloves, minced
1 c. slivered almonds
1 c. carrots, sliced
1 c. celery, sliced
1 c. red peppers, sliced

1 c. green peppers, sliced
1 c. green onions, sliced
1 c. mushrooms, sliced
¼ c. Bragg's liquid aminos
hot cooked rice
1 c. broccoli, cut into pieces (about
  1 inch)

Sauce

⅓ c. Bragg's liquid aminos
1 ½ c. water
3 T. arrowroot powder or cornstarch

1 tsp. honey
1 tsp. chicken style seasoning
⅛ tsp. cayenne pepper (optional)

In a heated fry pan or wok place Bragg's liquid aminos, garlic, and tofu, cook until slightly browned, then place this mixture in a separate bowl. In the same fry pan or wok, saute in oil, the almonds, carrots, and celery for 2–3 minutes. Add broccoli, onions, mushrooms, and peppers, continue stir frying for 2–3 more minutes, until crisp.

Sauce: place all ingredients in a blender in the order as listed and blend well. Add the tofu mixture and sauce to the vegetables, heat until bubbly and thickened. Serve over hot rice.

Basic Bread Dressing

½ c. oil or water
½ c. chopped onion
½ c. chopped celery
1 T. parsley, dried
1 tsp. salt
½ tsp. sage
4 c. dry bread crumbs (about 12 slices)

Saute onion and celery in oil or water in a large skillet. Add parsley, salt, sage, and bread crumbs, toss lightly. Bake in 7 x 7 inch dish or loaf pan (coated with oil spray) at 350° F for 35–40 minutes.

Vegetarian Chili

3 cans kidney beans
1 c. bulgur or cracked wheat
1 ½ c. chopped onion
2 c. chopped tomatoes
1 c. chopped carrot
1 c. chopped celery
1 c. chopped green pepper
2 c. tomato sauce
1 T. cumin
1 tsp. basil
1 T. garlic powder
4 c. water

Place beans, water, vegetables, and seasonings in a large pan and cook until vegetables are tender. Then add bulgur or cracked wheat and cook an additional 15–20 minutes.

Curried Rice

½ c. water	1 c. water
1 lg. onion, chopped	1 can tomatoes (optional)
1 T. curry or substitute	2 potatoes, diced
1 tsp. tumeric	½ c. peas
1 tsp. garlic powder	1 c. cauliflower
1 tsp. ginger	Hot cooked rice

Saute onion in ½ cup water. Then mix curry, tumeric, garlic powder, and ginger with 1 cup of water. Add to onions and cover. Simmer for 5 minutes. Add potatoes, peas, cauliflower, and tomatoes and bring to a boil. Place in casserole dish and bake at 350° for 30 minutes. Serve over rice.

Spinach Calzones

½ lb. mushrooms, sliced or chopped	1 tsp. salt
1 pkg. Mori-nu tofu, mashed	1 tsp. garlic powder
1 T. chicken-style seasoning	1 tsp. Italian seasoning
1 lg. onion, chopped finely	Bread dough—1 loaf from favorite recipe
1 pkg. frozen chopped spinach, thawed and drained	Spaghetti sauce

Calzone—the dough should have risen for the final time. Roll out thin. Cut into 6 inch circles. Mix mushrooms, tofu, spinach, onion, and seasonings together. In each circle, place ⅓ cup of filling. Fold dough over & seal edges to make a half-circle. Repeat until dough & filling are gone. Place on a cookie sheet. With a pastry brush, brush water on the top of each calzone, bake at 350° for 25–30 minutes. Top with spaghetti sauce before serving.

Vegetable Curry with Rice

1 ½ c. uncooked rice	1 tsp. salt
5 ½ c. water	1 tsp. cumin
4 T. flour	Dash cayenne pepper (optional)
½ c. water	1 lg. onion, chopped
1–2 T. oil or water	3 garlic cloves, minced
2 T. curry or curry substitute	

10 sm. new red potatoes, cut in 1 inch cubes
2 pkgs. George Washington broth or vegetable broth
2 c. carrots, cut into 1 inch pieces
3 c. broccoli florets
2 c. cauliflower florets
1 med. red bell pepper, chopped
1 med. green bell pepper, chopped
1 lb. tofu, cut into 1 inch pieces

Cook rice in 3 cups of the water. Meanwhile, in a small bowl, combine ½ cup of water and flour, beat until smooth, set aside. Heat oil or water in a large saucepan over medium heat, until hot. Add curry powder, salt, cumin, and cayenne. Cook and stir 1 minute. Add onion and garlic, cook and stir 1–2 minutes. Add potatoes, broth, carrots and remaining water. Bring to a boil. Reduce heat, Cover and simmer for 10 minutes. Add broccoli, cauliflower, peppers, and tofu. Cover and simmer for 5–6 minutes or until vegetables are crisp. Stir flour mixture into the above and cook over medium heat until mixture boils and thickens, stirring constantly. Cook for an additional minute. Serve over hot cooked rice.

Tip: Freeze rice, beans, and non-cream based soups for quick preparation on a later date.

Kidney Bean Chili

8 c. cooked kidney beans
1 qt. tomatoes
16 oz. tomato sauce
4 med. onions, chopped fine
4 cloves garlic, minced
1 med. green pepper, chopped (optional)
3 c. water
½ c. lemon juice
2 T. oregano
1 T. cumin
1 ½ tsp. sage
1 tsp. salt

Place all ingredients in a large pan and simmer for 30–45 minutes. May place in a crock pot on low and it will be ready for you when you get home from work.

Spinach Rice Casserole

3 c. cooked rice
1 10-oz. pkg. frozen chopped spinach
1 ½ c. tofu
1 c. water
1 c. onion, diced
½ lb. non-dairy cheese, grated
2 tsp. Bragg's liquid aminos
½ tsp. salt
½ tsp. thyme
½ tsp. rosemary
½ tsp. marjoram
¾ c. bread crumbs

Thaw spinach and squeeze out excess moisture. In a blender, combine tofu and water, blend until creamy. Place ¼ cup of bread crumbs aside. Mix all ingredients (except the bread crumbs set aside) together. Pour mixture into an oiled or sprayed casserole dish. Sprinkle remaining bread crumbs on top. Bake at 350° for 1 hour, or until inserted knife blade comes out clean.

Veggie Meatless Balls

1 ½ c. bread or cracker crumbs
⅓ c. pecan meal
3 T. parsley, dried
1 lg. onion, finely chopped
¾ tsp. cumin
1 tsp. basil
¾ tsp. oregano
3 T. Bragg's liquid aminos
¾ c. water
1 T. chicken style seasoning
3 T. flax seed
Tomato/pasta sauce

Combine bread crumbs and nuts. In water or oil saute onion, then add cumin, basil, oregano, chicken-style seasoning, parsley, and liquid aminos. In a blender, place water and flax seeds, blend for 2–3 minute, scraping down the sides as needed. The mixture becomes very thick. Place this in a glass bowl (or small sauce pan if using the stove), making sure to get as much off the sides of the blender as possible, then cook in microwave or on stove for 1 ½–2 minutes. When mixture is cooked add to the bread crumb mixture and stir well. Form balls, using a tablespoon and place on a cookie sheet. Bake at 350° for 20–30 minutes. Place meatballs in favorite heated tomato/spaghetti sauce just before serving.

"Let nutrition be your medicine."
—Hippocrates

Main Dishes

Easy Bean Casserole

8 oz. baked tortilla chips, crushed
4 c. pinto beans
32 oz. tomato sauce (4 cups)
¾ c. water
⅔ c. sliced black olives
1 c. finely chopped onions

In a large bowl, place beans, olives, crushed tortilla chips, tomato sauce, onions, and water. Mix well together. Save a few olives to garnish the top. Place in an oil sprayed casserole dish and cover with foil Bake at 350° in a preheated oven for 50 minutes.

Rice and Bean Burritos

4 c. cooked beans
  (kidney, red, black or pinto)
1 c. cooked rice
1 c. bulgur wheat reconstituted
  in ¾ c. hot water
1 medium onion, chopped
1 clove garlic, crushed
1 tsp. garlic powder
1 tsp. onion powder
2 tsp. cumin
1 T. sage
1 c. salsa (mild, medium or hot)
1 ½ c. tomato sauce
8 tortillas

Saute onion and garlic in a small amount of water or oil, until tender. Then mix all the seasonings, beans, rice and bulgur wheat with the onion and garlic. Wrap tortillas in aluminum foil and bake at 350° for 15 minutes. Spoon rice and bean mixture in the center of the warmed tortillas, fold into a burrito shape. Place folded burritos in a 13 x 9 inch baking dish. Mix salsa and tomato sauce and spoon on top of burritos. Cover and bake at 375° degrees for 45 minutes.

Spinach Stuffed Shells

2-10 oz. pkgs. frozen chopped spinach
1 lb. water packed tofu
2 c. non-dairy mozzarella cheese
1 pkg. jumbo shells
salt to taste
Pasta Sauce (see This & That)

Prepare spinach as directed on the package, drain, press out excess liquid. Pour into a large bowl and cool slightly. Stir in cheese, tofu, and salt. Fill each cooked shell with about a tablespoon of filling mixture.

Preheat oven to 350°. Spoon pasta sauce evenly in a 4-quart roasting or Pyrex pan, arrange filled shells in sauce. Cover the pan with foil and bake for 30 minute or until hot and bubbly.

Spinach Stuffed Shells II

2 lbs. tofu (or 3-12 oz. boxes) crumbled
2 T. dried parsley
½ tsp. basil
½ tsp. oregano
1 tsp. garlic powder
1 ½ tsp. onion powder
1 ½ tsp. salt
¼ tsp. Italian seasoning
1-10-oz. box frozen chopped spinach, thawed and drained
1 box jumbo pasta shells (cooked as per package instructions)
Pasta Sauce (See This & That)

Mix together tofu, salt, and seasonings. Fill each cooked shell with about a tablespoon of filling mixture. Preheat oven to 350°. Spoon a small amount of pasta sauce evenly in a 4-quart roasting pan. Arrange filled shells in sauce. Pour remainder of sauce over shells. Cover the pan with foil and bake for 30 minutes or until hot and bubbly. Special thanks to Roberta Yeagley for this recipe.

Vegetable Burritos

1 clove garlic, crushed
1 medium onion, chopped
1 8-oz. can water chestnuts, drained and chopped
1 large zucchini, coarsely shredded
1 c. fresh mushrooms, sliced
1 medium tomato, chopped
1 red sweet bell pepper, chopped
1 c. fresh or frozen corn
1 tsp. celery salt
salt to taste
10 flour tortillas
1 medium avocado, chopped
1 c. tofu sour cream (see This & That)
1 T. lemon juice

Sauté first 10 ingredients in a small amount of water or oil, until tender. Then mix together tofu sour cream, lemon juice and avocado. Warm tortillas by wrapping tightly in aluminum foil. Bake at 350° for 15 minutes. Remove foil from tortillas. Spoon vegetable mixture in the center of each warmed tortillas. Fold into a burrito shape. Place burritos in a 13 x 9 inch baking dish and bake at 350° degrees for 15 minutes. Top with sour cream/avocado sauce.

Variation: Add 1 cup cooked rice and/or 1 cup non-dairy cheese to vegetable mixture before folding into a burrito.

Baked Beans

8 c. cooked great northern beans
1 medium onion, chopped fine
½–1 c. tomato sauce or ketchup
½ c. succanat or molasses

Place all ingredients in bowl and mix well. Place in either a baking dish or crock pot and cover. Bake for 1 hour at 350° or put the crock pot on a low temperature, cook all day and the beans will be ready for dinner when you get home from work.

Bean Patties

½ lb. extra-firm tofu, crumbled
1 ½ c. instant potato flakes
2 c. cooked beans or lentils
½ c. oatmeal
1 medium onion, chopped fine
1 T. molasses
½ tsp garlic powder
½ tsp. basil
1 T. minced dried onions
1 T. Bragg's liquid aminos
1 ½ T. chicken style seasoning
½ tsp. salt

Saute onion in a small amount of water or oil. Mash tofu with a fork and mix the remainder of the ingredients into tofu (including the onion), making a fine crumble. The mixture should be moist but not wet. Form into burger shapes and place on a cookie sheet. Bake at 350° for 20 minutes, turn over and continue baking for another 15 minutes. These freeze well and can be made ahead of time. Serve in a sandwich or with a favorite gravy.

Soybean Patties

1 c. soybeans
1 ¼ c. water
3 T. Bragg's liquid aminos
½ tsp. salt
¼ tsp. garlic powder
¼ tsp. Italian Seasoning
1 T. parsley

1 ⅓ c. quick oats
⅔ c. pecan meal
1 small onion, diced fine
1 garlic clove, minced or pressed

Place the first 7 items in a blender and blend well. Place the quick oats in a bowl and pour blended mixture over them. Add remaining ingredients and mix well. Let mixture sit for 5 minutes to absorb the liquid. In a nonstick sprayed frying pan make patties about 2 inches in diameter. Patties will be soft, but will firm up. Cover and fry 5–7 minutes, turn over and fry another 5–7 minutes. You may bake on a cookie sheet in a 350° oven for 20–30 minutes if preferred.

Fettuccini Alfredo

2 red sweet bell peppers, cut in strips
6 green onions, chopped
¼ c. pine nuts
¾ c. raw cashews
1 ¾ c. water
1 T. flour

1 T. chicken-style seasoning
1 tsp. salt
1 tsp. oregano
¼–½ c. fresh parsley
1-8 oz. pkg. fettuccini noodles

Cook fettuccini according to directions on package. Toast pine nuts in a dry skillet until slightly browned. Saute peppers (about 4 minutes) in a small amount of water or oil, then add onions and saute for another 3 minutes. Place cashews, water, flour, and seasonings in a blender. Process until very smooth. Pour into a sauce pan and simmer over medium-low heat until thickened. Add sauteed vegetables, pine nuts, and fresh parsley, cook another 4–5 minutes. Toss noodles with Alfredo sauce. Serve immediately.

Tip: To snip and measure fresh parsley (or any fresh herb) in one step. Wash fresh parsley and place in a measuring cup. Snip parsley in the cup with scissors until the desired amount is reached.

"People need loving the most when they deserve it the least."

Desserts

"Whether therefore ye eat or drink,
or whatsoever ye do,
do all to the glory of God."

1 Corinthians 10:31 KJV

Cherry Almond Cookies

¼ c. ground flax seed
½ c. boiling water
½ c. raw cane sugar crystals
1 tsp. almond flavoring
¾ tsp. salt
1 tsp. aluminum-free baking powder
⅓ c. canola oil
1 c. flour
1 ½ c. oatmeal
1 c. shredded coconut
1 c. dried cherries
1 c. sliced almonds

First mix flax seed and water in a small bowl and let it stand.

Mix together all other ingredients, except flour. Add flax seed and mix well. Add flour and stir until well moistened. Drop by teaspoonful onto an oil-sprayed cookie sheet. Bake at 350° for 10–12 minutes.

Variation: delete cherries and almond flavoring and use ½ cup dried pineapple diced, ½ cup golden raisins and 1 tsp. vanilla.

Unbaked Peanut Butter Fudge Cookies

1 c. peanut butter
½ c. honey
2 tsp. vanilla
½ tsp. salt
2 c. oat flour
  (whiz oatmeal in blender)

Mix together all ingredients until well moistened and dough sticks together in a ball. Pinch off pieces and roll into 1 inch balls and place on waxed paper. Flatten cookies with a fork to approximately ¼ inch thick. Makes 2 dozen cookies.

Variation: Press dough into an 8 x 8 inch square pan. Top with melted carob chips and cut in squares.

Pineapple Rice Pudding

1-12.3 oz. box silken tofu
1 c. pineapple, crushed or tidbits
4 c. cooked rice
¾ tsp. salt
⅓ c. honey
½ c. chopped nuts (optional)
1 tsp. vanilla extract
½ tsp. cardamom
½ tsp. coriander

Drain pineapple and reserve liquid. Pour tofu, salt, honey, coriander, cardamom and reserved pineapple juice in blender and blend until very smooth. Place rice, pineapple tidbits, and walnuts in a large mixing bowl. Add tofu mixture and stir until all ingredients are well coated. Place pudding in a covered serving dish. This may be served warm or refrigerated. Makes a quick and easy breakfast dish if made the night before.

Variation: add ½ c. golden raisins.

Yellow Delicious Pie

6 med to large yellow delicious apples, peeled (optional) and sliced
½ c. cane juice crystals
1 tsp. coriander
½ tsp. cardamom
¼ c. unbleached flour
¼ tsp. ginger
1 recipe oatmeal pie crust

Roll out ½ of the pie crust recipe and place in an 8 or 9 inch pie pan. Arrange apples on the crust. In a small bowl combine the cane crystals, flour, coriander, cardamom, and ginger. Mix well, then sprinkle evenly over the apples. Roll out the top crust and cover apples, crimp or flute edges. Make several small slits in top crust to let steam escape. Bake at 350° for 1 hour. Serve with favorite cream topping. Serves 6–8.

Variation: This basic recipe works with most fruit, use 3–4 cups of fruit.

Oatmeal Pie Crust

1 ½ c. oatmeal
½ c. unbleached flour
1 tsp. salt
⅓ c. oil
⅓ c. water

Whiz oatmeal in a blender to make oat flour. Pour into a bowl and add unbleached flour, salt, oil, and water. Mix together until well moistened. Divide in half and roll out each piece of dough between 2 pieces of waxed paper. This recipe makes 1 two-crust or 2 onecrust pies.

Unbaked Carob Brownies

3 ¾ c. graham cracker crumbs
1 ½ c. pecan meal
¾ c. coconut, shredded
1 c. soy milk

2 tsp. vanilla
¼ tsp. almond flavoring
2 ¼ c. carob chips

Combine the coconut, pecans, and graham cracker crumbs in a bowl, mix well. Next, place the vanilla, almond flavoring, milk, and carob chips in a sauce pan or in the microwave and melt together. Add this mixture to the graham cracker crumb mixture. Mix well, press into an oil sprayed 9 x 13 inch pan. Refrigerate for at least 30 minutes before serving. Cut and serve.

Smoothies

2 bananas, chunked and frozen
1 c. blueberries, frozen
1 c. soymilk
1 c. ice cubes

2 tsp. vanilla
½ c. juice (optional) orange, white grape

Place all ingredients in blender and process until very smooth. Makes approximately 4 servings. Enjoy!

Variations: Mix and match any frozen fruit or juice.
   Add ½ c. tofu.
   Add 1–2 T. nuts per serving.

Coconut Chip Cups

Filling

1 ½ c. boiling water
4 T. Emes kosher-jel
   (unflavored vegetable gelatin)
¾ c. raw cashews
¼ tsp. coconut extract
1 ½ tsp. vanilla extract
1 tsp. almond extract

1 ½ tsp. lemon juice
⅓ c. pineapple juice
¼ tsp. salt
¼ tsp. orange flavoring
1 c. coconut milk
¼ c. honey

Blend the above ingredients until smooth. Then add: coconut milk and honey. Blend again until smooth and place in the refrigerator to gel.

Crust
2 c. graham cracker crumbs
½ c. honey

Stir together, place in cupcake papers and press crumbs down firmly, with the bottom of an oiled glass. Bake 350° for 5–8 minutes, until golden brown. Let cool for 10 minutes. Place 1 ½–2 Tablespoons filling in each cup.

Topping
2 c. unsweetened coconut
¾ c. carob chips

Toast the coconut on a cookie sheet until golden brown. Sprinkle cups with toasted coconut and carob chips.

Lemon Dessert

2-12.3 oz. boxes tofu (extra firm)
3 fresh lemons
2 T. honey
1 pkg. Mori-nu instant pudding mate, lemon flavor
Graham cracker crust

Squeeze juice from 3 lemons. Place lemon juice, tofu, and honey in a blender, mix well until smooth. Add lemon pudding, mix and blend again until mixture becomes smooth. Pour into a graham cracker crust and chill.

Graham Cracker Crust

2 c. graham crackers crushed
⅓ c. soy margarine (may substitute oil)
1 T. ground coriander

Mix graham crackers, soy margarine, and coriander together, and press in sprayed pan.

Oatmeal Carob Cookies

3 c. oats
2 c. flour
1 c. unsweetened coconut, shredded
⅔ c. raisins
⅔ c. carob chips
1 c. chopped nuts (optional)
1 tsp. salt

1 tsp. coriander
½ tsp. cardamom
1 T. EnerG Egg replacer
1 ⅔ c. soy, rice, or nut milk
½ c. oil (can substitute applesauce)
⅔ c. honey
2 tsp. non-aluminum baking powder

In a large bowl, mix together dry ingredients. In a small bowl mix egg replacer with milk until no lumps remain. Add oil and honey. Pour this mixture into the dry ingredients. Mix well. Place by tablespoonfuls onto an oil-sprayed cooking sheet. Bake at 350° for 18–20 minutes until lightly browned. Remove and cool.

Layered Fruit Bars

Base layer:
    1 c. unbleached flour
    1 ½ c. oatmeal
    ½ tsp. salt
    ½ cup raw cane sugar crystals (divided)
        reserve 2 T.
    ⅓ c. canola oil
    3 T. water

Middle Layer:
    1 ¼ c. (1 10-oz. jar) "all fruit" jam

Top Layer:
    ⅓ c. unbleached flour
    1 c. shredded coconut
    1 c. chopped walnuts
    2 T. raw cane sugar
    1 tsp. ground coriander (optional)
    3 T. water
    pinch of salt

Combine base layer ingredients. Press firmly and evenly into an oil-sprayed 9 x 13 baking pan. Spread fruit jam over the entire base layer. Mix together top layer ingredients. Sprinkle over fruit layer and lightly pat into the jam. Bake at 350° for 20–25 minutes. Cool slightly before cutting into bars.

Filling Variation: Simmer 1 ¼ c. chopped dried fuit (dates, raisins, apricots, etc.) in ¾ c. water or juice for several minutes until thickened.

Pumpkin Bars

Use basic Layered Fruit Bar recipe (above).

Pumpkin filling
1 ½ c. pure maple syrup
1 c. firm or extra firm tofu
¼ c. corn starch
1 ½ tsp. coriander
¾ tsp. cardamon
¾ tsp. ginger
¾ tsp. salt
2 T. vanilla
1-15 oz. can pumpkin

In blender, combine all ingredients except pumpkin. Blend until smooth. Pour into bowl and add pumpkin. Mix well. Pour over base layer of recipe and continue with instructions for top layer. Bake at 350° for 30–35 minutes.

Heavenly Cheesecake

Crust
1–1 ½ c. graham cracker crumbs
½ c. oil or non-hydrogenated soy butter

Filling
24 oz. non-dairy cream cheese substitute, plain
¾ c. milled cane sugar
1 T. vanilla
1 tsp. almond
4 T. lemon juice
2 T. EnerG Egg Replacer
1 ½ T. Emes plain kosher jel
Dash of coriander

Sour Cream Mixture
8 oz. non-dairy sour cream substitute
3 T. fructose

Blend graham crackers and ½ c. oil or non-hydrogenated soy butter together and place in a spring-form pan. Bake 10–15 minutes at 350° until crust is golden, let cool. For filling blend non-dairy cream cheese and milled cane sugar together, then add vanilla, lemon juice, EnerG egg replacer, Emes kosher jel and coriander and mix well. Pour into baked crust. Bake at 350° for 25 minutes or until an inserted cake tester or knife comes out clean. Then mix the sour cream and fructose well . Pour over baked cream cheese mixture. Bake for 8 more minutes at 350° (or until cake tester comes out clean) and remove from oven. Let cool and serve plain or add a berry topping of your choice.

Note: The "Tofutti" brand non-dairy substitute seems to give this recipe the best taste. And though you might use other substitutes, even the best cheesecake connoisseurs won't know this is vegan.

Pineapple or Strawberry Tapioca

¼ c. minute tapioca
2 c. canned pineapple, (drained & reserved) or fresh strawberry slices
Pineapple juice and water to make 2 cups
¼ tsp. salt
⅓–½ c. milled cane sugar or honey

Heat liquid to boiling, sprinkle in tapioca. Reduce heat and simmer until tapioca is transparent, stirring frequently. Remove from heat and add sweetener and salt. Partially cool, then carefully fold in fruit. Chill. Thanks to Marilyn Anderson for this recipe.

*"A happy home is where both mates think they
got better than they deserve."*

This & That

"Use the talents you possess;
for the woods would be silent if only the best birds sang."

—Unknown

Bedda Chedda Cheese Sauce

½ c. raw cashew pieces
1 c. very hot water
½ c. pimentos
¼ c. nutritional food yeast flakes
1 tsp. salt
2 T. lemon juice
2 ¼ c. hot cooked rice
1 c. water

In blender process cashews and 1 cup of very hot water. Blend until smooth. Add pimentos, food yeast, salt, and lemon juice, and blend until smooth. Add rice, and remaining water and continue to blend until very smooth. If you like a thicker consistency, add less water at the end or if you like it thinner, add more water.

Use this sauce over pasta, baked potatoes, vegetables, etc. For a great chip dip, add a small jar of your favorite salsa (do not blend salsa).

Chik Seasoning

½ c. nutritional yeast
1 T. onion powder

½ tsp. each: tumeric
garlic powder
marjoram
summer savory
sage
celery seed

1 ½ T. dried parsley

Combine all ingredients except parsley in a blender or seed grinder. Process until powdered. Stir in parsley. Pour into a jar with a tight-fitting lid. Store in the refrigerator or freezer.

Use Chik Seasoning to season soups, stews, potatoes and other vegetables, burgers, broth, gravy, etc.

Tip: Use more herbs to season your food and cut back on the salt.

Freezer Spaghetti Sauce

20 large tomatoes
3 large onions
4 large carrots
2 large green bell peppers
½ c. parsley, dried
2 T. Italian seasoning
1 T. honey
1 T. salt

Cut up tomatoes, onions, peppers, and carrots, place in a large pan with parsley, honey, and salt. Bring to a boil and then simmer for 30 minutes. Place in a blender and puree. Cool. Place in containers to freeze. Thanks to Becky Abbott & Carol Guild for this idea.

Tofu Sour Cream

1 pkg. firm or extra firm (silken)
¼ c. water
1 tsp. salt
2 tsp. lemon juice

Process all ingredients together in a blender until smooth. Chill until ready to use.

Pasta Tomato Sauce

2 T. oil or water
1 sm. onion, diced
1-28 oz. can tomatoes
1-6 oz. can tomato paste
1 T. honey or milled cane sugar
1 tsp. oregano
salt to taste

In a 3 qt. sauce pan over medium heat, cook onion in oil or water until tender, stirring often. Add tomatoes with their liquid, tomato paste, honey, oregano, and salt to taste. Reduce heat to low, cover, and simmer 20–30 minutes to blend flavors.

Slaw Dressing

1 lb. Tofu
1 T. Braggs Liquid aminos
Juice of 2 lemons
1 tsp. dill weed
½ tsp. basil
¼ tsp. salt
2 T. honey
⅓ c. raw cashews

Place all ingredients in a blender and whiz until smooth. If you want a smoother consistency add 2 T. water.

Thousand Island Dressing

1-8 oz. can tomato sauce
½ c. raw cashews
2 T. lemon juice
2 tsp. honey
1 tsp. salt
1 ½ tsp. onion powder

1 tsp. paprika
1-12.3 oz. box firm silken tofu
 (about 1 ½ cups)
2 small green onions, finely diced
1 T. dried parsley

Place all the ingredients, except parsley and green onions in blender and blend until very smooth. Pour into bowl and add parsley and green onions. Stir until well mixed. Cover and chill.

Variation: Add chopped pimento, olives, or pickles to taste.

Nut Milk

⅔ c. raw almonds or cashews
¼ tsp. salt
1 tsp. vanilla

1 T. honey
4 c. water

In blender process nuts with a small amount of the water until very smooth. Add salt, vanilla, and honey. Continue blending for a minute or two. Add remaining water. Pour into a pitcher, cover and refrigerate. Stir well before serving.

Spinach Dip I

1-10 oz. pkg. frozen chopped spinach
 (thawed & drained)
12 oz. firm tofu
1 pkg. Knorr dried vegetable soup mix
½ c. Non-dairy mayonnaise

⅓ tsp. garlic powder
1 small can water chestnuts
 (chopped)
1/4 c. chopped green onion or chives

Blend tofu, mayonnaise, & garlic powder until smooth. Add remaining ingredients, mix well. Chill at least 1 hour before serving, but best if chilled overnight. Serve with crackers or bite-sized pieces of dark bread.

Spinach Dip II

- 1 lb. firm tofu
- 1 small can water chestnuts, finely chopped
- 1 10-oz. package chopped frozen spinach, thawed and drained
- ¼ c. green onions, finely chopped
- 6 baby carrots, quartered lengthwise and finely chopped
- 1 tsp. dill weed
- ½ tsp. celery seed
- 1 tsp. dried parsley
- ⅛ tsp. tumeric
- 1 tsp. salt
- ¼ tsp. garlic powder
- 2 T. potato flour
- Non-dairy mayonnaise

Blend tofu with a small amount of soy milk until smooth. Pour into a large bowl. Add water chestnuts, spinach, onions, and carrots. Mix well. Add seasonings, and potato flour. Stir again, then add enough of your favorite non-dairy mayonnaise to make the mixture a good dipping consistency. It is best if it is chilled for several hours or overnight. Serve with bite size pieces of dark bread or your favorite crackers.

Taco Dip

- 1 can vegetarian refried beans
- 1 c. non-dairy plain cream cheese
- 1 c. non-dairy sour cream
- 2 c. non-dairy shredded cheese, cheddar flavored or Bedda Chedda Cheese (see This & That)
- ½ c. black olives, sliced
- 1 pkg. taco seasoning mix
- ½ c. chopped green onions
- 2 large ripe tomatoes, finely chopped

Spread beans evenly on the bottom of a 9 x 9 baking pan. Mix together cream cheese, sour cream, and taco seasoning mix. Spread mixture over beans. Layer tomatoes, then olives, and then green onions. Cover with cheese. Warm thoroughly in oven at 325° for 20 minutes. Serving suggestion: Can also add avocado (but if you do, do not let it bubble because it will ruin the avocado).

Pet Treats

2 c. whole wheat flour
2 c. white unbleached flour
1 c. cornmeal
½ c. ground flaxseed
1 tsp. garlic powder

¼ c. Chik Seasoning
   (This and That, p. 66)
¼ c. olive oil
2 ½ warm water

Mix dry ingredients together in a large bowl. Add oil and water. Stir until well-blended and moist. Roll out as cookie dough on a floured board. Cut into desired shapes with cookie cutters or a knife. Place on oil-sprayed baking sheet and prick each treat with a fork several times to prevent bubbling. Bake at 300° for 40 minutes. Remove from baking sheet and place on rack or waxed paper to cool until hard and dry.

Variation: Use beef flavoring instead of chicken.

> "True religion and the laws of health go hand in hand.... The things of nature are God's blessings, provided to give health to body, mind, and soul. They are given to the well to keep them well and the sick to make them well."
>
> —E. G. White, *My Life Today*, 35.

SEASONINGS

Seasonings are an important part of cooking. They add flavor and savoriness to your recipes. But not all seasonings are alike, some can act as irritants to your body. The most common problems caused are to your gastrointestinal system. But in some individuals, they can also increase blood pressure, nerve irritation, and food cravings. Listed below are some non-irritating seasonings, some substitutions for some irritants, and common seasonings to use with different vegetables.

Non- Irritating Seasonings

Basil
Dried leaves of the herb *Osimum basilicum.*, a member of the mint family. A favorite in tomato dishes, pizza, and the primary ingredient of pesto sauces. Also used with green Thai curry.

Bay Leaf
Bay Leaves or Laurel, are the dried leaves of the evergreen tree, *Laurus nobilis*. They have a distinctively strong, aromatic, spicy flavor. Bay Leaf is the approved term for this spice, but the name "laurel" is still seen frequently. Used in soups, stews, tomato dishes.

Caraway
Caraway Seed is the dried fruit of the herb *Carum carvi*. The small, tannish brown seeds have a flavor similar to a blend of Dill and Anise—sweet but faintly sharp. It is known for its flavor in rye bread, and it is used to flavor cakes, biscuits, cheese, carrot, and potato dishes.

Celery Seed
Celery seed is the dried fruit of the *Apium graveolens* which is related, but not identical, to the vegetable celery plant. The tiny brown seeds have a celery-like flavor and aroma. Adds zest to salads, such as cole slaw, potato salad. Use in stews, soups, tomato dishes and cooked vegetables. Celery is naturally high in sodium and is a good choice for someone on a salt restricted diet.

Eden's Bounty

Cardamom Cardamom is the dried, unripened fruit of the perennial *Elettaria cardamomum*. Enclosed in the fruit pods are tiny, brown, aromatic seeds which are slightly pungent to taste. Used in pastries, Middle-east, African, Asian, and Indian cooking.

Cilantro Cilantro is a member of the parsley family. The leaf of the coriander plant, it is spicy in flavor and pungent in aroma. It is also known as Chinese parsley. Used primarily in Oriental and Mexican dishes.

Coriander Coriander is the dried, ripe fruit of the herb *Coriandum sativum*. The tannish brown seeds have a sweetly aromatic flavor which is slightly lemony. It is a member of the parsley family and has a mild, distinctive taste similar to a combination of lemon peel and sage. Add to curry, legumes, onions, potatoes, and baked goods. Coriander is actually thought to increase the appetite.

Chives Chives, *Allium schoenoprasum*, are the reed-like stems of a perennial, bulbous plant of the lily family. The name "Chives" is derived from the Latin *cepa*, meaning onion. Chives are a member of the onion family. Use in soups, sauces, dips, potatoes, and as a garnish.

Cumin Cumin is the dried seed of the herb *Cuminum cyminum*, a member of the parsley family. Cumin is a key component in both Chili Powder and Curry Powder. Cumin is used frequently in Mexican, Thai, Vietnamese, and Indian cuisines. Adds flavor to chili and bean dishes.

Dill Seed Dill is an annual of the parsley family and is related to Anise, Caraway, Coriander, Cumin, and Fennel. Dill Weed is the dried leaves of the herb *Anethum graveolens*, the same plant from which Dill Seed is derived. Use dill to season soups, tomato juice beverages, rice pilaf, salads, legumes, and breads.

Fennel Seed	Fennel is the dried, ripe fruit of the perennial *Foeniculum vulgare*. The taste is similar to licorice. Use with a variety of dishes, such as entrees, salads, potatoes, and pastries.
Garlic	Garlic is the fresh or dried bulb of the *Allium sativam*. It is used widely with soups, dips, entrees, salads, and vegetable dishes. Can use either garlic powder (1/4 tsp = 1 garlic clove) or fresh garlic. Either mince or press the fresh garlic cloves.
Marjoram, Sweet	Marjoram is the dried leaves and floral parts of the herb *Origanium hortensis*. Most scientists consider Marjoram to be a species of Oregano. Tastes a little stronger and sweeter than thyme. Use to flavor soups, vegetables, especially green vegetables and tomatoes, bread dressings, and salads.
Mint	Mint leaves are dried spearmint leaves of the species *Mentha spicata*. The dark green leaves have a pleasant warm, fresh, aromatic, sweet flavor with a cool aftertaste. Commonly used in Middle-East dishes. Can be used with eggplant, peas, tomatoes, and potatoes.
Oregano	Oregano is the dried leaves of the herbs *Origanum spp* or *Lippia spp* (Mexican). The Mediterranean variety is closely related to Marjoram and is very similar in physical appearance. "Oregano" means Marjoram in Spanish. Commonly used as a salt replacer. Use it on Mexican or Italian type dishes, such as burritos, lasagna, and/or pizza. It goes with most tomato dishes and also makes a great topping for vegetable type sandwiches.
Paprika	Paprika is the dried, ground pods of *Capsicum annum*, a sweet red pepper. It is mildly flavored and prized for its brilliant red color. Use with soups, green vegetables, sauces, potato salad, cole slaw, and stews. High in vitamins A and C. An attractive garnish on potatoes and salads.

Eden's Bounty

Parsley Parsley is the dried leaves of the hardy biennial herb *Petroselinum crispum* (family *Umbelliferae*). This is probably the most well-known and used herb in the United States. Parsley adds color, and thus visual appeal, to many foods. It is used in salad dressings, soups, sauces, tofu, and vegetables, especially carrots. And it is high in vitamin C.

Poppy Seed Poppy is the dried, kidney-shaped seed of the annual *Papaver somniferum*. The seeds are very small in size, slate blue in color and are nut-like in flavor. It is used topically on breads and rolls and added to vegetables and salad dressings.

Rosemary Rosemary is the dried leaves of the evergreen *Rosmarinus officinalis*. It is native to the Mediterranean area. Nicely flavors tomato dishes and sauces, spinach, peas and potatoes. Commonly used to flavor breads and rice.

Saffron Saffron is the dried yellow stigmas of the violet flowers of *Crocus sativus*, a member of the Iris family. Saffron is mainly used as a colorant and flavoring for pastry and rice.

Sage Sage is the dried leaves of the herb *Salvia officinalis*. The aromatic leaves are silvery gray in color. Adds zest to breads, tofu, casseroles, stuffings, tomatoes, eggplant, lima beans, and especially bean soup.

Savory Savory is the dried leaves of the herb *Satureja hortensis*. The brownish-green leaves are fragrantly aromatic, resembling that of Thyme. It is commonly called summer or garden savory. Has a bitter flavor but enhances vegetables, salad dressings, stuffing, tofu dishes and legumes.

Sesame Seed Sesame is the dried, oval-shaped seed of the herb *Sesamum indicum*. Sesame Seed is harvested by hand. The seeds have a rich nut-like flavor when toasted. Sesame Seed contains 25 percent protein. It is also high in calcium. Used to add texture and flavor to a variety of breads, rolls, crackers, and salad dressings.

Tarragon Tarragon is the dried leaves of the herb *Artemisia dracunculus*. The slender dark-green leaves have a pleasant anise-like flavor and aroma. Used with soups, spread, salad dressing, celery, beets, peas, potatoes, tomato dishes, and in vegetable juices.

Thyme Thyme is the dried leaves of *Thymus vulgaris*, a small perennial of the mint family. The leaves measure about one quarter of an inch in length and one tenth of an inch in width. Can be used with most soups, tomato juice, tomato sauces, tofu, and vegetables.

Turmeric Turmeric is the dried root of the plant *Curcuma longa*. Noted for its bright yellow color, it is related to and similar in size to ginger. Turmeric's flavor resembles a combination of ginger and pepper. Used primarily as a natural coloring agent, it also gives a distinct tart, bitter flavor when blended into sauces and dressings. It is the main ingredient for color and taste in curry powder. Use with rice and anything where you may want a curry type flavor.

Eden's Bounty

Common Irritants

Allspice
Baking soda & most baking powder
Cinnamon
Cloves Curry
Ginger Mustard Seed
Nutmeg
Pepper (black & white)
Salt
Vinegar

Baking Soda/Powder Substitute
  Use 1–2 teaspoons baking yeast dissolved in ¼ cup of warm water and sweetened with 1/2 teaspoon honey. Baking yeast is high in B vitamins.

Cinnamon Substitute
  2 parts of coriander to 1 part of cardamom. Grind/blend together finely and use in recipes calling for cinnamon.

Nutmeg
  Substitute cardamom on a 1:1 ratio.

Vinegar
  Substitute lemon juice on a 1:1 ratio

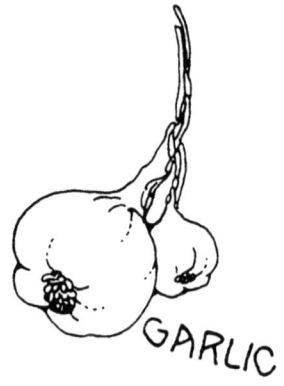

"Garlic...a remedy for all diseases and hurts."
—Nicholas Culpepper, 1643

Vegetable Seasonings

Artichokes	Dill
Asparagus	Caraway, chives, lemon juice, marjoram, savory, sesame seeds, sweet basil, tarragon, thyme.
Beans (dried)	Bay leaf, cumin, dill, garlic, marjoram, mint, oregano, savory, sweet basil, thyme.
Beans (snap)	Dill, marjoram, oregano, savory, sweet basil, thyme.
Beets	Bay leaves, celery seed, dill, lemon or orange juice, savory, sweet basil, tarragon, thyme
Breads	Caraway, coriander, dill, fennel, garlic, marjoram, parsley, poppy seeds, rosemary.
Broccoli	Caraway, dill, lemon juice, marjoram, oregano, tarragon
Brussel sprouts	Caraway, dill, marjoram, sage, savory, sweet basil, thyme
Cabbage	Caraway, celery seeds, dill, garlic, sage, savory, tarragon.
Carrots	Bay leaves, caraway, curry, dill, fennel, lemon or orange peel, marjoram, mint, parsley, sesame seed, sweet basil, thyme.
Cole slaw	Caraway, dill, marjoram, mint, savory.
Corn	Chives, garlic, paprika, pimento, savory, turmeric.
Cauliflower	Caraway, celery seeds, dill, paprika, oregano, rosemary, savory, sesame seed, tarragon.
Cucumber	Dill, parsley, savory, basil, tarragon.
Eggplant	Dill, marjoram, mint, oregano, parsley, rosemary, sage, sweet basil, thyme.
Fruits	Caraway, coriander, fennel, mint, rosemary, sesame seeds.
Green beans	Celery seeds, dill, marjoram, rosemary, sage, savory, sweet basil, tarragon, thyme.

Eden's Bounty

Lima beans	Chives, marjoram, oregano, parsley, sage, savory, sweet basil, tarragon, turmeric.
Okra	Garlic, parsley, sweet basil.
Onions	Caraway, celery seeds, oregano, parsley, sage, sweet basil, thyme.
Parsnips	Bay leaves, caraway, curry, dill, fennel, marjoram, mint, parsley, sweet basil, thyme.
Peas	Dill, marjoram, mint, oregano, parsley, poppy seeds, rosemary, sage, savory, sweet basil, thyme.
Potatoes	Bay leaves, caraway, celery seeds, chives, dill, marjoram, oregano, paprika, parsley, poppy seeds, rosemary, savory, sweet basil, thyme.
Rice	Saffron, sesame seeds.
Squash	Garlic, nutmeg
Spaghetti sauces	Garlic, oregano, sweet basil
Spinach	Garlic, lemon juice, marjoram, oregano, rosemary, sweet basil, tarragon, thyme
Tomatoes	Celery seed, curry, dill, garlic, parsley, sweet basil, tarragon, thyme.
Turnips & Rutabagas	Caraway, garlic

Cooking Times for Grains

Grain (1 cup dry)	Water	Cooking Time in Minutes	Yield in cups
Barley (whole)	3 cups	45	3 ½
Brown rice	2 cups	40	3
Buckwheat groats (kasha)	2 cups	15	3
Bulghur wheat	2 cups	12–15	2 ½
Cracked wheat	2 cups	15–25	2 ⅓
Coarse cornmeal (polenta)	4 cups	25	3
Millet	3 cups	30–45	3 ½
Oats, regular rolled	2 cups	5–8	2
Oats, quick-cooking	2 cups	1–3	2
Oats, steel-cut	2 ½ cups	15–20	3
Rye berries	3 cups	60	2 ½
Rye, cracked	2 ½ cups	10–15	2 ⅔
Triticale berries	3 cups	45	3
Wild rice	2 cups	60	3
Whole-wheat berries	3 cups	60+	2 ⅔

Herbs & Natural Remedies

"Pure air, sunlight, abstemiousness, rest, exercise, proper diet, the use of water, trust in divine power—these are the true remedies."

Ministry of Healing, 127

Introduction

At the end of creation week, "God saw everything that He had made, and, behold it was very good." (Genesis 1:31, KJV) Soon after, sin entered the world and with sin came sickness, disease, pain, and suffering. Our loving God did not leave us without remedies for these ailments. In addition to the 8 natural laws of health. He gave us herbs and plants with medicinal properties in them. The herbs of the field can be powerful healing agents and are available to everyone, no matter what one's economic status. You can create your own herbal preparations. Most are simple to make and as effective as those you buy. The following material provides a description of some of the most common terms used in herbal preparations, a list and description of commonly used herbs, how to gather, dry and store herbs, and recipes for making teas, baths, syrups, oils, tablets, poultices, and salves.

There are also sections on using activated charcoal and water (both inside and out) as natural remedies. The most important addition to each treatment is God's blessing.

Remember to always ask Him to guide and bless your attempts at using His methods of natural healing.

The information in this book should not be substituted for that given by a qualified healthcare practitioner. Information is only given as a general guide. Study the herbs and remedies you wish to use and make wise choices based on that knowledge. Learn all you can about a treatment and its contraindications before putting it into practice. If purchasing herbs in pill or capsule form, look for labels that say "Standardized". Check dosages and warnings on every bottle. Be cautious, as some remedies may cause unwanted reactions because of allergies, drug interactions, or certain chronic health problems. The authors and publishers accept no responsibility for misuse of any information.

Commonly Used Herbs

Calendula (*Calendula officinalis*), also known as pot marigold, should be in every garden. This easily grown annual makes a pretty border and is used for both medicinal and culinary purposes. Plants begin blooming in late spring and will continue to put out blossoms until late fall. Its bright yellow and orange flowers add color and flavor to salads and other dishes. Medicinally, the flowers are used in teas, tinctures, ointments, salves, and other preparations. Calendula is said to be anti-inflammatory and anti-viral, acting as a stimulant to the immune system and promoting wound healing. It is used to make a gargle for mouth/ throat infections, and a crushed flower rubbed on an insect sting or bite can bring quick relief. Salves and ointments are used for sunburn, scrapes, rashes (including diaper rash), and other skin ailments. Those with allergies to ragweed and other asters should use caution but generally no adverse side effects occur.

Chamomile, German (*Matricaria recrutita*) is also known as wild chamomile. It is a hardy annual that grows up to 24 inches high. Dried or fresh flowers from this plant are used most often for medicinal purposes. Roman **Chamomile** (*Chamaemelum nobile*) also known as garden chamomile is an evergreen perennial that grows about 4 inches high with 10 inch flower stems, which can also be used medicinally. Chamomile has been used internally to relieve nausea, colic, headaches, insomnia, and stress. Used as a mild tea, it acts as a soothing sleep aid for children. External preparations can reduce inflammation and help to heal cuts and bruises. Chamomile is an herb that has very few unfavorable side effects. However, persons allergic to ragweed, and other plants in the aster family should use chamomile with caution.

Catnip (*Nepeta cataria*) Also known as Cat Mint works as a mild sedative. It is a wonderful herb to use for colic and stomach ache. Catnip compresses on the forehead help to overcome headaches and a quart of strong tea added to a warm bath may alleviate the pain of menstrual cramps. Drink 1 cup up to 3 times daily. For colic, give tea by a dropper or put a small amount in the baby's bottle. Check 'dosage' in the glossary for giving the proper amount.

Cornsilk (*Zea Mays*) The soft little hairs surrounding the ear of corn in the husk make a pain relieving remedy which soothes the urinary tract. A diuretic, corn silk is traditionally used to treat bladder, kidney, and problems that cause painful urination. No known contraindications.

Echinacea (*Echinacea Augustifolia*), also known as purple coneflower, is mostly used to boost the immune system to ward off the symptoms of colds and flu. It also helps to overcome sore throats when made into a gargle. Usually, the dried root is made into a decoction, but leaves and flowers are sometimes used with good success. Caution: Persons allergic to aster family plants may have adverse reactions to Echinacea. Also, the German Commission E recommends that those with auto-immune diseases such as tuberculosis, multiple sclerosis, and HIV, do not use Echinacea.

Elderberry (*Sambucus canadensis*) **and** (*Sambucus nigra*) are great immune-boosting herbs that grow throughout the USA Elderberries are said to be antibacterial, antifungal, antiviral, and anti-inflammatory. The dried flowers, made into tea, are great for treating fevers, flu, colds, bronchitis. Elder flowers have also been used in eye compresses and washes, as well as in various skin preparations. Extracts made from dried berries are used for cold & flu treatments and also for preventative measures. Elderberry syrup is frequently recommended as a cold and flu remedy and used to alleviate nausea and calm the stomach. Fresh berries make wonderful jams and pies. Caution: Always use dried or cooked parts of the Elder bush. Raw parts may cause adverse reactions.

Fenugreek (*Trigonella foenum-graecum*) seeds are traditionally used either whole or powdered to help lower cholesterol and lower blood sugar. Some women drink the tea to reduce menopausal hot flashes. Externally they can be made into a poultice. Because of the high mucilagin content fenugreek could interfere with other treatments by preventing absorption of other drugs. It should not be used by pregnant women.

Feverfew (*Fanacetum parthenium*) has great anti-inflammatory properties and the flowers and leaves are said to help relieve arthritis pain. However, it is best known for its powerful action on headaches. It may take up to 6 weeks to make a noticeable difference in headache control, but worth the wait in most people. Fresh leaves are very bitter and may cause mouth ulcers. Do not use during pregnancy.

"If you are not ready to alter your way of life, you cannot be healed..."
—Hippocrates

Garlic (*Allium sativum*), also known as Russian penicillin, is a widely grown herb. Traditionally the clove or bulb has been used to prevent illness as well as cure. It has more than 160 compounds in its chemistry and is said to be anti-bacterial, anti-fungal, anti-parasitic, and anti-inflammatory. It helps to prevent colds, flu, and some cancers. Garlic has been found helpful in lowering blood pressure, cholesterol, and triglycerides in the blood. Oil of garlic can be used to treat earache. Use caution if taking blood thinners.

Ginger (*Zinbabar officinale*) fresh and dried roots are used for treating an upset stomach, nausea, motion sickness, and stimulating the appetite. It is also said to help reduce blood cholesterol. Persons with gall bladder disease should avoid ginger. Ginger is a blood thinner. Use caution if on medications for that purpose.

Hawthorn (*Crategus oxyacantha*), also known as May Blossom Tree, helps to alleviate high blood pressure and dilate coronary and peripheral arteries. Chemical compounds in the berries are strengthening to the heart as well. Some claim they lower cholesterol. A decoction of the berries may also help in cases of insomnia. There are no known side effects.

Lavender (*Lavandula augustifolia*) Its blossoms produce a lovely oil that has virtually unlimited uses. A few drops of the essential oil may be added to massage oils, perfumes, topical pain relief oils (as for headaches and burns), potpourris, insect repellents and more. The dried flowers are used to make great teas, compresses, hot foot baths, sleep pillows, facials, steam, and beautiful bouquets.

Lemon Balm (*Melissas officinalis*) is a perennial garden herb in the mint family. Dried leaf preparations include teas and creams. Internally it is used for digestive upsets, and insomnia. External creams are used for treating cold sores and to inhibit bacteria and fungi. According to some studies, herpes lesions heal much quicker when a 1% extract cream is applied. No contraindications are noted.

Milk Thistle (*Silybum marianum*) seeds have traditionally been used to make a tonic for liver disorders. This herb can be used to treat hepatitis, cirrhosis, and other chronic diseases. There are no known side effects.

Mullein (*Verbascum thapsus*) grows wild throughout North America. The dried leaves are used in an infusion for upper respiratory congestion. It can also be made into a salve for wound healing. The yellow flowers made into an infused oil make a wonderful earache treatment. No contraindications.

Peppermint (*Mentha Xpiperita*) leaves have been used for many years for relief of nausea, colds, headaches, and cramps. The essential oil is said to be anti-bacterial, and anti-viral. It also helps relieve muscle spasms. Do not use peppermint if you have Acid Reflux Disease, as it opens the lower esophagus and seems to make it worse.

Plantain (*Plantago major* or *P. Ianceolata*) is also known as White Man's foot. It is within everyone's reach. It grows everywhere and is very advantageous fresh as well as dried and made into various preparations. Crush fresh leaves to relieve pain from insect stings. Tea is used for upper respiratory tract infections. Salves can bring relief to skin ulcers, eczema, scrapes and cuts. It has mild antibiotic and anti-inflammatory properties. Generally there are no adverse side effects.

Red Clover (*Trifolium pratense*) blossoms can be found growing everywhere in the continental United States. Red clover is known as a great blood purifier. It is believed to stimulate the immune system and is sometimes used in alternative cancer therapies. Red clover is one of the richest sources of phytoestrogenic isoflavones and therefore used to treat menopausal symptoms such as hot flashes. No side effects have been reported for Red Clover. Drink freely.

Shepherds Purse (*Capsella bursa-pastoris*) is a member of the mustard family. The whole dried plant is used to make a tea or tincture. Traditionally it has been one of the best herbs for stopping internal bleeding. External bleeding has been alleviated with a poultice, or ointment. For earache, crush a plant to pulp and squeeze several drops of juice in the ear, or you could try stuffing the plant pulp up a nostril to treat a nose bleed.

Slippery Elm (*Ulmus rubra*) Also known as Red Elm is very soothing for gastrointestinal irritations such as ulcers and colitis. The inner bark of the tree with its high mucilage content is also an excellent treatment for sore throats.

St. Johns Wort (*Hypericum perfatum*) Aerial parts and particularly flowers are used to treat various ailments. St. Johns Wort has very good reports for treating mild depression when standardized capsules are taken. Infused oils and salves are excellent for injuries, burns, and other wounds as it has anti-bacterial action. Hypericin in the flowers can cause fair skinned people to break out in blisters if exposed to excessive sunlight. Take proper precautions if using St. Johns Wort preparations.

Stinging Nettle (*Urtica disica*) in the growing state, definitely sting if touched by the bare skin. Always wear gloves when collecting. Nettle has many medicinal uses and is also used as a culinary greens dish. Nettle is very high in calcium and iron and is used to treat anemia. It is traditionally used as a blood purifier and urinary tract cleanser. A nettle compress helps relieve painful joints and infusions increase milk flow in lactating mothers. Recent research finds that nettle root combined with saw palmetto to be very useful in treating Benign Prostatic Hyperplasia (BPH). No adverse side effects reported other than the "sting" when touching fresh leaves. There is no sting in dried or cooked plants.

Tumeric (*curcuma Tonga*) is a member of the ginger family. The dried ground root is used both medicinally and as a culinary herb. Externally it is used for ringworm, wounds, insect bites, and bleeding. Internally it treats ulcers, atherosclerosis, arthritis, inflammation and more. There are no side effects as a general rule, but should be avoided if gallstones are present.

Yellow Dock (*Rumex crispus*) also known as "Sour Dock and Curly Dock." The root is used medicinally. It is taken internally as a laxative, blood purifier, and for thyroid dysfunctions. Yellow dock is also used as an alternative cancer remedy. Ointments and salves are applied topically for skin eruptions, cuts, bruises, athlete's foot, hemorrhoids, plantar worts, and more. Avoid use during pregnancy.

Glossary

Aireal	Parts of the plant above the ground.
Alcohol	The alcohol used in making herbal medicine is always GRAIN alcohol. Alcohol is not always recommended as a solvent for preparations. Vegetable glycerin is a good alternative. However, if the tincture or extract being used is made with alcohol as the solvent, the alcohol can be evaporated out very quickly. Simply place the tincture dosage in a cup and add a little boiling water. Let stand for 5 minutes before drinking.
Bark	Outside covering of the trunk of trees or branches.
Bath Tea	An infusion to add to the bath water.
Carrier Oil	The oils used to dilute essential oils or to make infused oils.
Capsule	A gelatin or vegetable gelatin casing in which to place herbs for easier swallowing.
Compress	A cloth dipped in water or a strong infusion, with most of the liquid squeezed out and then applied to the skin.
Decoction	A tea made with roots, woody stems, and bark.
Dosages	Clark's Rule of dosages goes on the theory that most herbal dosages are calculated for an adult man who weighs 150 pounds. Dosages for men, women, and children weighing more or less can easily be calculated using the following formula: $$\frac{\text{Weight of individual}}{150 \text{ (average adult weight)}} = \text{Amount of dose}$$
Essential Oils	Extremely concentrated plant oils removed by distillation. Most should not be used internally without advice from a professional. Externally most should be diluted.
Extract	A preparation made by soaking herbs in solvents to withdraw the medicinal properties from the plants.

Glycerite	A tincture using glycerin as the menstruum. A good ratio is 2 parts of glycerin to 1 part of water.
Infused Oil	This is made by soaking herbs in a vegetable (carrier) oil to extract their medicinal properties.
Infusion	Also known as tea or tesane. An infusion is made by placing the lighter parts of a plant such as leaves, blossoms, and fruit in boiling water and allowing it to steep for 15–20 minutes. Drink 1 c. 2–3 times a day.
Menstruum	An extracting solution.
Poultice	A soft, moist, plant or charcoal based preparation applied to an area of the body to help alleviate pain or to draw out infection and inflammation. It works best if warmed and left on for several hours or overnight.
Root/Rhizome	The underground part of a plant.
Salve	A solid or semisolid, healing ointment for wounds and sores.
Standardized	When buying encapsulated or tablet herbs, this means that the herb has a specific amount of whatever medicinal constituents are believed to be the healing properties of the plant.
Steep	To soak.
Syrup	A thickened, sweetened form of making herbal medicines. Good for working with bitter herbs and also getting children to take herb preparations more easily. Great for sore throats and coughs.
Tea	Infusion.
Tesane	Tea, infusion.
Tincture	A solution made by soaking herbs in solvents (alcohol, glycerin and/or vinegar) to draw out the medicinal, useful compounds of a plant—a concentrated extract.

Eden's Bounty

Vegetable Glycerin   A sweet mucilagninous constituent of oils of plant origin. In addition to being a great solvent for tinctures and extracts, glycerin is a wonderful skin softener.

What is an herb?
>*"The friend of thy physician and the praise of cooks."*
>—Charlemagne

Gathering, Drying, and Storing Herbs

When gathering the aerial parts of an herb, remember that most plants have maximum medicinal potency just before they bloom or on the day of blooming. Morning is the best time to gather herbs—just after the dew has dried and before the sun gets too hot.

If gathering roots, it is best to collect them when the sap is just beginning to rise in the spring or in the fall when the sap has gone down to the roots. Wash the roots to remove all traces of dirt, then slice thinly and dry thoroughly on a screen with good air flow.

Bark like slippery elm and wild cherry is harvested by stripping off the outer bark and shaving lengths of inner bark. Cut the bark into small pieces for complete drying. Dry on a screen in a shady place with a good air flow.

Seeds can be gathered anytime after ripening, before they fall to the ground. Lay them out on a tray for a day or two to make sure they are completely dry.

A shady place with good air flow is best for drying leafy plants and flowers. A simple way to dry them is to tie bunches of a dozen or so stems each (more or less depending on the size of the stems) with heavy string leaving a length of string about 2 feet long connected to the herbs. Punch a small hole in the bottom of a brown paper bag. Place the herbs in the bag and run the string out through the bottom of the bag. Tie the string around a tree branch so the herb bag hangs upside down. Air can flow around the herbs to speed drying and the bag keeps them clean while they are drying (see following page for illustration).

Drying of herbs may also be done in a food dryer. A machine with multiple heat settings is recommended. Aireal herbs should be dried at 85°–95° and roots/bark at about 125°.

Oven drying is also possible. Set your oven at the lowest temperature. Spread herbs thinly on a cookie sheet and place in the oven. You may need to prop the oven door open a bit to maintain the proper temperature. Caution: keep small children/pets away from the oven if the door is open. It takes about 5 hours to dry herbs in your oven.

Eight pounds of fresh herbs = approximately 1 pound of dried herbs.

All the dried herbs are best stored in air tight glass containers in a cool dark cupboard. If stored in sunlight they will lose their potency in a short time.

To store whole-leaf culinary herbs in the freezer, rinse leaves thoroughly and dry between layers of paper towels. Then layer them in a covered container between sheets of waxed paper or parchment. Freeze up to six months. Or, you can chop the herbs finely. Fill ice cube trays with the herbs and cover with water. Freeze. When frozen, empty the trays into plastic zipper bags and return to the freezer. When herbs are needed for cooking, just drop a cube or two into the soup, casserole, etc.

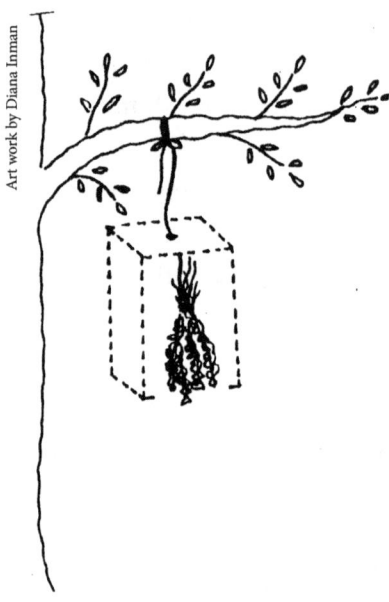

Art work by Diana Inman

Tip: When gathering herbs don't collect them near roadside or sprayed fields as they may be contaminated by exhaust fumes or pesticides. Do your gathering 100 or more feet from these areas. The further the better.

TEAS, OILS, & SYRUPS

Basic Herbal Tea

1–2 tsp. dried herb 1 c. boiling water
1 tsp. honey of other sweetener (optional)

Put herb and sweetener in a sturdy mug. Fill mug with boiling water, cover, and let steep for 15 minutes, strain & discard herbs. Drink 2–3 cups daily. Store the remainder in the refrigerator, but do not keep more than 2–3 days.

Elder Flower Tea

2 tsp. dried crushed, elder flowers 1 tsp. honey (optional)
1 c. boiling water

Pour boiling water over dried herb and let steep 20 minutes. Drink up to 3 cups a day. Used for colds, flu, fever, bronchitis and more.

Chamomile Tea

1 heaped tsp. flowers 1 c. boiling water

Pour boiling water over dried flowers, steep for 15 minutes. Drink freely as needed up to five times a day. Helps with insomnia, indigestion, nausea, inflammation, respiratory problems.

Cornsilk Tea

⅓ c. dried or ⅔ c. fresh cornsilk 2 tsp. honey (optional)
4 c. boiling water

Pour boiling water over cornsilk and steep until cool enough to drink. Used to treat bladder, kidney, & other problems that cause painful urination. At first sign of discomfort, drink a cup of tea and one cup every hour for 3 hours. Then, drink as needed. No known contraindications.

Calming Tea

1 tsp. chamomile flowers
1 tsp. lemon balm leaves
1 c. water
1 tsp. honey

Bring water to a boil. Add herbs and remove from heat. Let steep for 15 minutes. This tea is relaxing for both children and adults.

Red Clover Tea

1 T. Red clover blossoms (dried/crushed)
1 tsp. honey (optional)
1 c. boiling water

Place clover blossoms and honey in a mug. Pour in the boiling water. Cover and let steep for 15–20 minutes. Red clover is traditionally used as a blood purifier, diuretic, and general tonic. It is rich in phytoestrogens and is sometimes used in alternative cancer therapies. Drink as freely as water.

Tea Pops

4 cups herbal tea
12 3-oz. disposable cups
12 popsicle sticks (available at craft stores) or plastic spoons

Make tea as directed. Strain if necessary. Pour tea into the cups. Insert popsicle stick or spoon. Place cups on tray and freeze. When frozen, store pops in re-sealable plastic bags or other air-tight container. When needed, remove pop from cup and enjoy. These are especially soothing for kids (of any age) suffering from sore throats. Variation: Make the tea more concentrated and add a bit of fruit juice to make pops more colorful. Or, make tea with juice instead of water.

Basic Decoction

3 T. dried herb (about 1 ½ ounces) bark, root, or stems
4 c. water
1 T. Honey (optional)

Chop or grind herbs. Place herbs and water in a stainless steel or glass pan. Bring to a boil. Turn down heat and simmer uncovered for 30-60 minutes. Remove from heat. Strain out herbs and discard. Add honey and stir until dissolved. Typical dosage is 1 c. up to three times a day.

Milk Thistle Decoction

2 T. dried crushed seeds
3 c. boiling water
2 tsp. honey

Pour boiling water on crushed seeds and simmer for 30 minutes. Cool and drink 1 cup, up to 4 times daily. Recommended for liver ailments.

Echinacea Decoction

4-6 T. dried Echinacea root, chopped or ground
4 c. water
Honey (optional)

Place herbs and water in a pan and bring to a boil. Lower heat and simmer uncovered for ½ hour. Strain the herb from the liquid. Add honey if desired. Drink 3–4 cups a day. Echinacea is used to stimulate the immune system. It works best if used on an "on and off" basis. At the first sign of a cold or flu, take echinacea for 7–14 days then take several days off from the treatment. Repeat for another 7–14 days if necessary and then stop taking it.

Tip: Make a large amount of medicinal tea at one time. When cooled, pour the extra in ice cube trays and freeze. When frozen remove from the trays and store in zipper bags in the freezer (up to several months). Thaw and use as needed.

Basic Infused Herbal Oil

3 parts ground herbs
4 parts extra virgin olive oil (or other carrier oil)

Put herbs and oil in a jar with a tight fitting lid. Shake to mix well. Place the jar in a warm spot and out of the direct sunlight for 2–3 weeks. Shake the jar daily to keep the herb well-covered with oil and to prevent mold from growing. When the infusion time is up, pour the oil through a fine strainer or several layers of cheesecloth or gauze to remove the herbs. Bottle the oil in glass jars and store in the refrigerator.

Speedy Infused Oil

3 parts ground herbs
4 parts olive or other carrier oil

Place herbs and oil in a crock pot. Once heated, simmer for 3-4 hours. Strain and store as in the Basic Infused Oil recipe. Check often to make sure mixture does not overheat and burn.

Basic Herbal Syrup

¼ c. dried herbs   1 c. honey
1 qt. water

Simmer herbs and water until mixture concentrates down to 1 pint. Add the honey and continue to simmer until thickened to desired consistency. Remove from heat and strain through a double layer of cheesecloth. Store in a glass jar in the refrigerator.

Honey-Lemon Cough Syrup

½ c. honey
¼ c. lemon juice

Mix together in a small saucepan. Heat until just at the boiling point. Remove from heat and cool. Take 1 teaspoonful as needed. Store in refrigerator.

Variation: Chop and saute one large onion in a bit of water until opaque. Add the honey and lemon juice and bring to a boil as above. Cool and blend in blender until smooth. Bottle, refrigerate, and use as needed.

Ellen's Cough Remedy

1 c. honey
5-10 drops eucalyptus essential oil

Place honey in small saucepan over medium heat until it boils. Simmer for several minutes. Remove from heat and stir in the eucalyptus oil. Mix well. Cool, bottle, and store.

"When the cough comes on, I take a teaspoonful of this mixture, and relief comes almost immediately. I have always used this with the best of results. I ask you to use the same remedy when you are troubled with the cough. This prescription may seem so simple that you feel no confidence in it, but I have tried it for a number of years and can highly recommend it."

—Ellen G. White (1909), *Letter 20*, Review & Herald Publishing.

Elderberry Syrup

1 c. dried elderberries Honey
2 c. boiling water

Place elderberries in a 1 quart jar. Pour boiling water over the berries. Cover and let steep for 8 hours. Pour mixture into a stainless steel or glass pan and simmer for 30 minutes. Strain out the berries and discard. Measure the liquid and add an equal amount of honey. Reheat and stir until honey dissolves. Cool. Pour into a clean glass jar. Seal tightly and store in refrigerator. For cold and flu prevention it is customary to take 2 tsp. of syrup twice a day. To treat an already acquired cold or flu the suggested dosage is 1 T. four times a day. It works best if treatment is started AS SOON AS SYMPTOMS BEGIN.

Elderberry Extract

3 c. dried elderberries, crushed
Menstruum: 2 parts vegetable glycerin and 1 part water

Place dried elderberries in a 1 quart jar. Add enough menstruum to fill jar. Cover tightly and shake well to cover all the berries. Let the mixture steep for 3–6 weeks, shaking once daily. Strain the extract through a triple layer of cheesecloth, squeezing out as much liquid as possible. Store in tightly covered glass bottle(s) in a cool, dark place. For the prevention of colds/flu, the traditional dosage is ½ tsp. of extract twice a day (may be stirred into a small mount of juice or water and drank). If treating colds/flu the suggested dosage is 1 tsp. four times a day.

Sore Throat Gargle

1 tsp. powdered ginger
1–2 T. lemon juice
1 tsp. honey
1 c. boiling water
A pinch of cayenne pepper (optional)

Place ginger, lemon juice, honey, and cayenne in a mug. Pour the boiling water over the mixture. Cover and allow to steep until warm. Gargle and swallow until gone. Repeat 2–3 times daily.

Variation: Cold pineapple juice can be gargled alternately throughout the day with the warm ginger tea for quick relief.

Tip: Gargles can also help to relieve earache pain.

BATHS, POULTICES, PILLS, LOTIONS & SALVES

Basic Herbal Bath

1 handful of dried herbs
  or 2 handfuls of fresh herbs
1 quart boiling water

Essential oil (optional)
Carrier oil or glycerin (optional)

Place the herbs in a muslin bag or a tube sock. Tie the top shut and place in a pan with the boiling water and let steep a minimum of 15 minutes. Add 6–8 drops of your favorite essential oil to the tea and a bit of carrier oil or glycerin for softening the skin. Pour contents of pan into a bathtub full of warm water. Soak in the tub for a minimum of 20 minutes. When finished bathing, remove bag/sock and discard herbs.

Caution: Be careful when oil is used, as it makes the tub slippery.

Calming Bedtime Bath Tea

¼ c. dried chamomile flowers
¼ c. dried lavender flowers
¼ c. dried lemon balm leaves

1 qt. water
Lavender essential oil

Bring water to a boil. Add herbs and remove from heat. Let steep for 20 minutes. Strain out herbs and discard them. Add several drops of lavender essential oil to the tea then pour it into a tub full of warm water. Soak in the tub at least 15–20 minutes. This is good for relaxing children at bedtime.

Note: If fresh herbs are used double or triple the amount of the dried herbs.

Oatmeal Bath

1 ½–2 c. oatmeal
½ c. calendula or chamomile petals (optional)

Put the oatmeal and herbs in a muslin bag and tie shut, or place them in a tube sock and tie a knot in the top. Place the bag or the sock in the tub while it is filling with warm water and leave it in while bathing. This bath is helpful for rashes and dry skin.

Optional: Add a few drops of your favorite essential oil to the bath.

Herbal Poultice

Ground herbs
Hot water

Combine enough dried or fresh ground herbs with hot water to form a thick paste. Then apply it to the affected area. Cover with gauze, a paper towel, or muslin. Place a piece of plastic over the poultice. (You can use a bread bag, or any type of plastic). Tape in place. To keep the poultice warm, use a heating pad or a hot water bottle, if desired. For maximum effect, leave the poultice on for several hours or overnight. See page 106 for illustration.

> "Many transgress the laws of health through ignorance, and they need instruction. But [most of us] know better than [we] do. [We] need to be impressed with the importance of making [the] knowledge [we have] a guide for [our lives]."
> —*Ministry of Healing*, 126.

Baby Care Tips

Diaper Rash: At first sign of rash begining, sit or hold the baby in a warm bath made with chamomile tea, calendula tea, or oatmeal (above) for about 15 minutes. Pat baby dry and spread a generous layer of calendula salve on affected area. Use the salve at each diaper change.

Cholic: A tea made from catnip is quite effective. Give tea with a dropper, or put a bit in the baby's bottle. Check "dosage" in the glossary (on p. 88) for giving proper amount. Remember babies are small, so they need to take only a small serving. Chamomile tea or a mix of chamomile and catnip is also helpful.

Herbs & Natural Remedies

Applying a Poultice

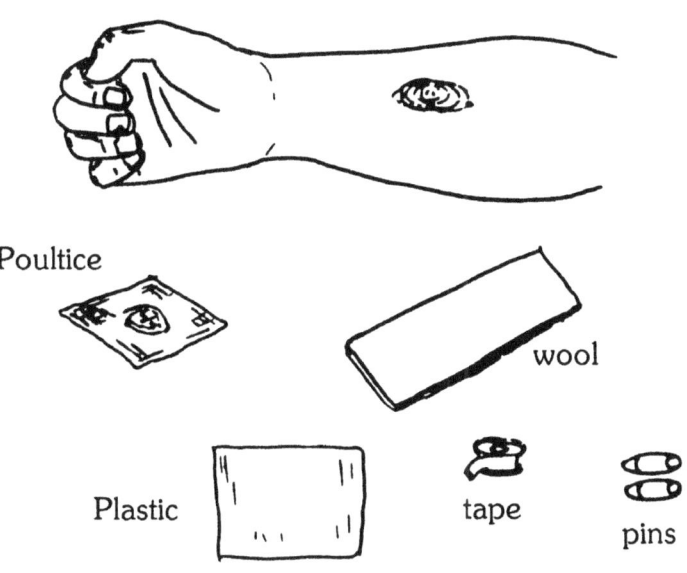
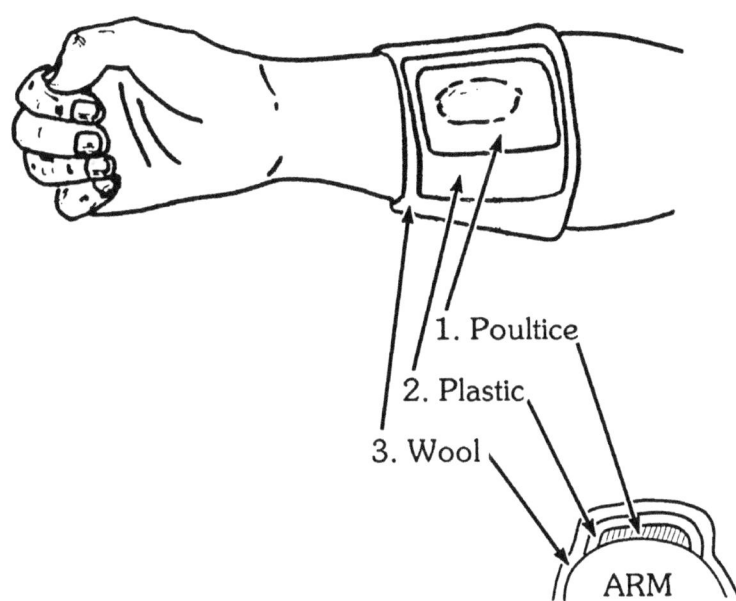

Reprinted from Clarence W. Dail, M.D. and Charles S. Thomas, Ph.D. (1989) *Hydrotherapy: Simple Treatments for Comomon Ailments*. Brushton, NY: TEACH Services, Inc. 77. Used by permission.

Onion Poultice

1 large onion, chopped coarsely
¼ c. flax seed, ground
2 T. olive oil

Place ingredients in a stainless steel or glass pan and saute until the onions are translucent. Wrap the onions and flax seed in cheesecloth or a large muslin bag and apply to the chest while still very warm. Cover with a towel and a hot water bottle or heating pad. Leave on for 20–30 minutes. This poultice eases cough, bronchitis, and pneumonia. It is safe to use on children.

Herbal Eye Compresses

2 chamomile tea bags
1 c. boiling water

Make an infusion by pouring the boiling water over the tea bags in a large mug. Let steep until cool. Squeeze excess liquid out of tea bags. Lie down in a comfortable spot. Put the tea bags on closed eyes and relax for 15–30 minutes. Eye compresses help to refresh the eye and reduce puffiness and itching.

Tip: Other eye treatments include slices of chilled cucumber for tired eyes and grated raw potato to help relieve puffiness. A 15–30 minute rest after each treatment is needed.

Easy Lip Balm

½ c. Almond oil or Infused Oil (see p. 95)
2 T. beeswax (1 oz.)
¾ tsp. lemon essential oil (optional)

Follow basic salve recipe (p. 104). A bit more beeswax may be necessary if using lip tubes instead of small jars. Add essential oil after wax has melted. Pour into containers and cool.

Tip: Try using lemon balm infused oil to treat "cold sores."

Herbal Compresses

Infusion/Decoction/Extract
Soft cotton cloth
Fabric to hold compress in place (optional)

Make a basic infusion/decoction/extract with the herbs of choice. When cool enough to handle, strain out and discard the herbs. Dip a piece of soft cotton cloth (size depends on area to be covered) in the liquid and wring lightly so it does not drip. Fold cloth several times to make a loose pad and apply to the skin. Leave on for at least 30 minutes.

Suggested Herbs for Compresses

Herb	Use	Temperature
Thyme	Skin infections	Warm
Lemon Balm	Chicken pox, herpes	Cool
Calendula	Acne, sunburn, skin ulcers, rashes	Warm or cool
Chamomile	Sunburn, rashes	Cool
Plantago	Pink-eye, skin ailments	Warm
Witch Hazel Extract	Hemorrhoid relief	Cold (keep in refrigerator)
Peppermint	Sinus pain	Cool

"Life in the open air is good for body and mind. It is God's medicine for the restoration of health. Pure air, good water, sunshine, beautiful surroundings, these are His means for restoring the sick to health in natural ways."

—E. G. White, *Manuscript 41*, 1902

Herbal Pills

Powered herbs   Water
Honey

Make your own herbal pills by mixing powdered herbs with enough honey and water to make a thick paste. Work the mixture until it is the consistency of thick cookie dough, adding more herbs or more liquid as needed. Knead it until smooth. Pinch off pill size pieces and roll into balls. Dry them on a cookie sheet at the lowest temperature in the oven or in a warm airy place. When thoroughly dried, store them in a glass container away from sunlight and moisture.

Basic Salve Recipe

1 c. infused herbal oil (p. 95)
¼ c. beeswax

Heat the herbal oil and beeswax together in a double boiler until the wax is melted. To test the firmness of the salve drop several drops into a cup of cold water. If you want it harder add a bit more wax, if softer, add a little more oil. When consistency is right, remove from heat and pour into small jars or tins. Store in a cool dark place.

Tip: For easy clean-up, put ingredients in a tin can set in a pan with 2 or 3 inches of water in it. Pinch can top to make an easy pour spout. Follow instructions, then dispose of can.

Poison Ivy or Poison Oak Lotion

½ tsp. salt   cosmetic clay
½ cup water   25 drops peppermint oil

Dissolve the salt in the water and add cosmetic clay until the mixture is creamy. Stir in about 25 drops of peppermint oil and apply to the affected area. For emergencies, add about 30 drops of peppermint oil to a full bottle of calamine lotion and shake well. Apply as needed. This lotion works very quickly.

Used with permission from Christopher Hobbs (1998). *Handmade Medicines*, 102.

Tip: Juice from the leaves/stems of Jewelweed (Impatiens pallida) also known as touch-me-not, can be applied as needed, especially during early stages of rash. In a hurry? Grind stems and leaves in blender.

CHARCOAL

Activated Charcoal is a powerful adsorbent. It is a harmless substance even when it is taken internally in large quantities and there are no ill effects when placed on the skin. It is also a great deodorizing agent. Charcoal has been used as a natural remedy for hundreds of years and listed in the United States as an official antidote since the 1800s. Activated charcoal is made by using a controlled burn of wood or bone and then subjecting it to steam or air at high temperature to activate it.

Charcoal can be purchased in powder, capsule, and tablet form with effectiveness being in that order. Capsules are approximately twice as effective as tablets.

Internally charcoal is used to treat such ills as: Poisoning or drug overdoses, diarrhea, nausea/vomiting, intestinal gas and bloating, liver and kidney diseases, and jaundice in newborns.

External poultices treat and adsorb the toxic effects of: Insect stings and bites, ear and eye infections, infectious bacteria and viruses, liver and kidney disease, toothaches and gum infections, skin infections, arthritis and other pain, and poison ivy. Poultices must be kept moist in order to do their work.

There are no conditions that will be made worse by using charcoal Even if it does no good—it will do no harm.

Cautions

1) A tattooing effect is possible if charcoal is placed on broken skin.

2) Food tends to interfere with internal adsorption so take charcoal between meals if possible.

3) Studies show that charcoal adsorbs many drug medications so allow some time between taking charcoal and other medications. It has been recommended that charcoal be taken one hour before or two hours after medications. <u>This includes drugs used for birth control.</u> Check with your physician.

Internal Dosages for Most Ailments

Adults:
1–2 T. charcoal
8 oz. water

Mix together and drink as needed to control symptoms

Children:
½ of the adult dose

Babies:
May be given charcoal water by an eye dropper or a nursing bottle

Charcoal Dosages for Poisoning

Estimated amount of poison of drugs taken	Charcoal to take if individual has not eaten in 2 hours	Charcoal to take if individual has eaten within 2 hours
1 teaspoon 1 or 2 capsules 1 or 2 tablets	1–2 tablespoons charcoal mixed in water. Drink all.	4–10 Tablespoons in 4 oz. water. Drink all and then fill glass with 8 oz. of water only and drink two more times.
1 Tablespoon 2 to 5 capsules 3 to 5 tablets	3–4 Tablespoons mixed in water. Drink all.	6–15 tablespoons in 8 oz. water. Drink all and then fill glass with 8 oz. of water only and drink two more times.
Unknown	1–5 tablespoons. Taken as above.	5–15 tablespoons. Taken as above.

Repeat all dosages in about 15 minutes and again if symptoms worsen. Contact your local health provider if unsure.

U.S. Poison Control Center Hotline—1-(800)-222-1222
Open 24 hours a day, 7 days a week.

Large Charcoal Poultices

2 c. ground flaxseed
2 c. activated charcoal powder
6 c. boiling water
Poultice pads

Carefully stir flaxseed (or other) and charcoal together. Slowly add boiling water and stir until smooth. (Spread on poultice material while warm. It will thicken as it cools. This recipe makes 8 poultices approximately 12" by 16".

For the large poultice, use disposable under pads (used for wheelchair or bed protection). They are normally about 2 feet by 3 feet in size and have 3 layers (the outer covering, the inner absorbent material, and the plastic backing). Decide what size body area the poultice will cover and then add several inches all around and cut the pad to desired size. Carefully peel back the top layer of the under pad from 3 sides. Spread poultice mixture on the pad about 1/4 inch thick. Replace the top layer over the charcoal. Seal edges shut with masking tape. Place on affected body part and hold in place with easily removed tape. Leave on for several hours or overnight for maximum effect. (See page 106)

Tip: Cornmeal, oatmeal, or cornstarch may be substituted for the ground flax seed.

Small Charcoal Poultices

2 T. ground flaxseed
2 T. charcoal powder
6 T. boiling water

Mix as in recipe for large poultices. Use a paper towel or cotton muslin or gauze instead of the under pad. Place the charcoal on one side of the paper towel. Fold the towel in half to cover charcoal. Place on affected are on the skin. Cover with a piece of plastic and tape in place. Leave on for several hours or overnight for maximum effect.

Tip: Poultices may be made ahead of time when they are needed often or on a daily basis. You may wish to have some on hand for emergencies also. Make the poultices as usual. Cover top layer with plastic wrap. Then carefully fold them in half with the charcoal side together. Then fold several times more and store in plastic zipper bags in the refrigerator for use in several days, or in the freezer for longer storage. Thaw at room temperature and warm in a microwave oven or over a heat register. Be careful because the plastic can get HOT!!

HYDROTHERAPY

Water—To Drink

Drinking adequate water is important to a healthy body. Many may wonder how much water one should really drink and what is the basis for that determination. Scientific studies now maintain that a good amount is 6–10 eight ounce glasses of water daily for the average adult. One way of figuring the body's need is to drink one—eight ounce glass of water for every 20 pounds of body weight, whether large or small. As we look at all the information, we may think how great it is that the study of science has figured all this out for us. However, the Bible writer, Ezekiel, had it all written down several thousand years ago. The following paragraphs are excerpted & revised from the book *Natural Alternatives* (1999).

How much water should I drink ?

God's word says: "Though shalt drink water by measure, the sixth part of an hin from time to time shalt thou drink." Ezekiel 4:11

Can we trust the word of God to answer this question? Let's look at this text a little closer, shall we? A hin is mentioned in numerous Old Testament Bible texts, such as Exodus 29:40; Leviticus 19:36, etc. Six hins equal 1 bath. The bath is about 10 gallons, having the same cubic contents as the ephah (Ezekiel 45:10, 11, 14) used in measuring substances. Now, let's do some math shall we? Remember, whatever $1/6$ of a hin is, we need to multiply it times two, from time to time."

- 6 hins = 1 bath
- 1 bath = 10 gallons
- 1 hin = 1.6 gallons
- $1/6$ hin = 34 oz. x 2 = 68 oz. = 8 ½ cups (approximately)

WOW! Now that we've answered that question, let's look at our body to see why God said eight (8) cups of water. Before this question can be answered accurately, one must first consider the term water balance. Water balance is simply when the total intake of water is equal to the total loss of water. Now this leads us to our next question. How much water do we lose each day? Our body loses 10 to 12 cups of water through urine, lungs, feces, and skin. Foods provide only two to four cups of water per day. Therefore, to maintain a water balance, (without engaging in vigorous exercise or sweating in high heat) we need to drink six to eight—8 ounce cups of water per day.

Due to the smelly, cloudy, and chlorine taste of tap water, many individuals are either choosing a water treatment system for their home, or buying bottled water. Listed below are definitions of various types of bottled water.

Reverse Osmosis	"fill-up" machines at your local (health food) stores is a process where water is forced through a very thin membrane to remove dissolved minerals. Water treated in this fashion is usually of very high quality.
Distilled water	This involves boiling water and then condensing and collecting the steam. IF done correctly, distilled water is usually of good quality, generally containing less than 10 parts per million (ppm) of dissolved solids.
Drinking water	It is required to meet the minimum health standards of the state or locality. You should read the label to determine which treatment methods have been used to produce the water.
Spring water	This comes from an underground formation (well/spring) in which water flows naturally to the surface-untreated. Public health authorities routinely find that as many as 10% to 40% of all private wells are contaminated with bacteria, chemicals, etc. If you get your water from a private well, please have it tested.
Mineral water	This is water which contains a high level (500 ppm) of total dissolved solids. There are no regulations regarding what these dissolved solids can be. Remember, practically any water can be called mineral water!

Note: Bottled water is required to meet essentially the same minimal EPA standards as public water systems. In fact, some bottled water is simply TAP WATER that has been bottled in another city. Therefore, contact your water service, health department, or outside source to test your water.

Used with permission from Eakins, C. M, and Eakins, P. A. (1999). *Natural Alternatives*. Huntsville, AL: Health Seminars Unlimited, 2-28, 2-29.

Water—To Treat

The science of using water for treating diseases and other ailments is known as hydrotherapy. During hydrotherapy, one may be sprayed, soaked, sponged, dipped, bathed, heated, cooled, or rubbed with ice. One may also be the recipient of irrigations, compresses, packs, steams, and frictions. All these treatments, when properly applied stimulate the nervous system in such a way that the recipient is often able to overcome the ailments that he has and to alleviate much pain and discomfort.

When performing hydrotherapy, always do it in a warm room which is free from drafts. Keep the recipient covered as much as possible to avoid chilling.

In the following pages, several simple home remedies using hydrotherapy are explained. As with all other treatments, always ask your heavenly Father to guide you and to use your knowledge and efforts to accomplish His will.

"The external application of water is one of the easiest ways of regulating the circulation of blood. A cold or cool bath is an excellent tonic. Warm baths open the pores and thus aid in the elimination of impurities. Both warm and neutral baths soothe the nerves and equalize circulation."

—Ellen G. White, *The Ministry of Healing*, 237.

Hot Foot Bath

The hot foot bath is a good all-around hydrotherapy treatment. It can be used alone or in conjunction with other treatments. The hot foot bath is known to increase white blood cell activity, thereby relieving many cold and flu symptoms, congestion in the head, pelvis, and chest, abdominal pain, and nosebleeds.

The heat from this treatment dilates the blood vessels in the feet causing blood from other parts of the body to move to the feet. It is that process that helps to relieve congestion in the upper parts of the body. The hot foot bath also warms the body and causes one to feel relaxed and comfortable.

Caution should be used if there is a loss of feeling in the feet or legs. If the patient has any vascular or circulatory problems, or if a diabetic. Check with your medical provider before proceeding.

Equipment needed:

- Foot basin
- Hot water (104°–110°), enough to cover ankles in basin
- Pitcher with additional hot water
- 1 T. dried mustard (optional)
- Bowl of ice water
- 2 wash clothes or hand towels
- 2 large towels
- Large blanket
- Large sheet
- Glass of water with a straw

Spread the blanket over the chair on which the patient will be sitting. Cover the blanket with a sheet. Have the patient sit on the chair and wrap them with the sheet and then the blanket. Be sure to cover snugly around the neck and knees to avoid air drafts.

If mustard is used, stir it into the foot basin filled with hot water. Then put the patient's feet in the basin and re-drape the blanket to cover the foot basin also.

As the patient begins to warm up, dip a washcloth/hand towel in the bowl of ice water. Wring out excessive water and place the resulting cold compress on the head. IF desired, use another cold cloth to wipe the face from time to time. Change the cold compress on the head every few minutes.

Add hot water to the footbath as needed to maintain the temperature. Frequently offer the patient water to drink during the treatment. Continue the hot foot bath for 20–30 minutes.

To end the treatment, hold the patient's feet a couple of inches out of the water with one hand and pour the bowl of ice water over the feet with the other. Dry their feet immediately and have them put on warm dry socks. The individual should then lie down and rest for a minimum of 30 minutes (1 hour is even better) after each treatment. If the patient perspires a great amount during the treatment and rest period, a warm bath or shower can be taken after the rest time.

Headache Treatment:

> *"When the head is congested, if the feet are put in a hot bath with a little (dried herb) mustard relief will be obtained."*
>
> —E. G. White, *Selected Messages II*, 297.96

Hot Foot Bath Illustration

Art work by Diana Inman

Heating Compress

The heating compress may be applied to the chest, feet, throat, joints, or abdomen. It is used to treat colds, flu, bronchitis, coughs, sore throats, insomnia, colic, pain, arthritis, constipation, and more. It is applied cold and as the body warms the compress it has a heating affect on the area treated. This draws the blood upward toward the skin surface and relieves deeper tissue congestion. It relaxes muscles and increases circulation much like a hot foot bath.

Heating Compress for the throat or elbow*

Heating Compress for the chest*

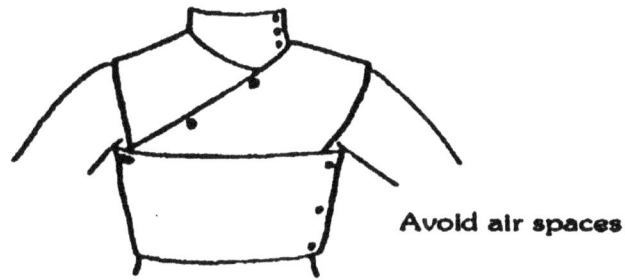

*Reprinted from Clarence W. Dail, M.D. and Charles S. Thomas, Ph.D. (1989) *Hydrotherapy: Simple Treatments for Common Ailments*. Brushton, NY: TEACH Services, Inc. 69. Used by permission.

Equipment needed:
- A piece of light weight cotton fabric to fit the area to be treated
- Plastic to fit over the cotton fabric
- Wool or synthetic fabric to cover the plastic on all sides by ½ to one inch
- Safety pins
- Cold water

Work in a warm room free from drafts. Make sure the patient is warm before starting the treatment. Dip the cotton fabric in the cold water and wring it out so there is no dripping. Place it on the body part to be treated. Cover the cotton fabric completely with plastic, leaving no fabric exposed. Wrap the wool/synthetic fabric over the first two layers. Pin it in place. Make the compress snug (but not tight) so air will be prevented from circulating under the compress. Leave the compress on for several hours or overnight. This may be repeated as needed.

Use caution with elderly or other patients who may not be able to produce enough heat to warm the compress. A heating pad or hot water bottle may be helpful in warming the compress in such a case.

Quick Tips for using heating compresses:

Throat: Use a wool sock if other wool is not available as a wrap.

Chest: Put on a wet, thin, sleeveless cotton T-shirt. Cover with a garbage bag (head & arms holes cut out) and pull on a wool/synthetic sweater.

Foot: Wet thin cotton socks. Slip feet into them and then in a plastic bread bag. Pull on a pair of wool socks. This treatment is especially good for treating colds.

Some practitioners don't use plastic between the fabric layers. Experiment on yourself to see which method you prefer.

Herbal Steam Inhalation

Herbs—fresh or dried
4 cups boiling water
1 large bowl
1 large towel or a sheet folded in quarters
Choose 1 or more herbs from among the following:

lavender	thyme	eucalyptus
mint	juniper	sage
rosemary	oregano	lemon balm

Place a large handful of fresh herbs or 4–6 Tablespoons of dried herbs in the bowl. Pour the boiling water over the herbs. Stir so that all the herbs are covered. Lean over the steaming bowl, covering both your head and the bowl with the towel or sheet (but not fully enclosed) for 15–20 minutes. Wipe face with a cold, wet cloth when finished. Repeat treatment 2–3 times daily. Breathing the steam from the aromatic herbs can help to relieve nasal, sinus, and lung congestion.

Steam Inhalation with Essential Oils

1 Qt. boiling water
5–10 drops essential oil
Follow procedure in Herbal Steam Inhalation.
Suggested decongestant oils are: Eucalyptus, lemon, lavender, peppermint, and pine.

Art work by Diana Inman

"There is health in the fragrance of the pine, the cedar, and the fir."
—E. G. White

Chair Steam Bath or Russian Steam Bath Equipment

- Simple straight chair
- Pot or kettle filled with water
- Hotplate
- Sheet, blanket, or fire-proof plastic cover
- Three towels, one for draping around the neck, one to turban the hair, and one for the seat
- Oral thermometer
- Ice bag
- Wrist watch or clock with a second hand
- Glass of water for drinking
- Hot foot bath equipment
- Oil of eucalyptus or mint if medicated steam is needed (about 1 teaspoon of oil or 2 tablespoons of dried mint leaves per pot of water)

Place hot plate and pot of boiling water under the chair seat. Fold a towel and place in the seat of chair. Put a tub of hot water in place for the hot foot bath.

Seat the undressed, turbaned patient on the towel and begin the hot foot bath. When sweating begins or oral temperature exceeds 100°, apply the cold compresses to the head. Keep the foot bath hot by adding more hot water.

Drape the sheet or blanket or both, or the fire-proof plastic cover in tent fashion around the back and shoulders to cover the body from the neck down, including the foot bath, so that the steam from the boiling pot is captured. Use care if a tea kettle is used that the spout is not directed toward the patient.

Fold a towel lengthwise and fashion as a snug-fitting collar to hold the sheet in place and prevent steam from escaping.

Encourage the patient to drink 1–2 glasses of hot water to encourage sweating. Check the oral temperature and pulse at temple or neck. Keep the pulse under 140 and the oral temperature under 104°. Keep the air temperature under the tent between 120° and 130° until the body temperature goes up to 102°–104°, when it can be reduced to 105°–110°.

After removing the steam apparatus and drying the feet, the sweating and fever can be prolonged by blankets, the patient going from chair to bed still wrapped in the tent sheet. Cover warmly with blankets to prolong the sweating. The treatment may be terminated with shower or cold mitten friction as desired.

Give one-half to one hour of reaction time in bed. If sweating has been profuse, have the patient take a cleaning shower at the end of the reaction time to cleanse the skin and readjust skin temperature. Administer copious amounts of water by mouth during and after the temperature.

This treatment helps to produce profuse sweating, opens up sinuses, and increases metabolism. It is useful in treating colds, influenza, rheumatoid arthritis, or a "crick" in the neck or back. It also helps to prepare a patient for a cold treatment.

Caution should be used when administering this treatment. The patient should not be debilitated or feeble. They should be vigorous and in good health. You need to keep a constant watch over the patient that their oral temperature does not go above 103° nor their heart rate above 140. Take the pulse and temperature every 15 minutes. If the temperature goes above 103° take their vital signs every 5 minutes. If the pulse exceeds 140, or if the temperature exceeds 104°, stop the treatment.

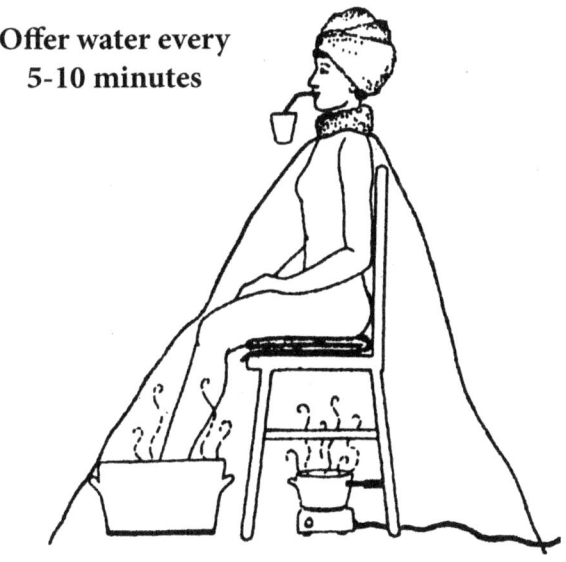

Used with permission from Drs. Agatha & Calvin Thrash (1981), *Home Remedies*, 72–3.

Eden's Bounty

Saltwater Nose Drops

1 c. warm water
1/4 tsp. salt

Dissolve salt in water. With a dropper put 2–3 drops of the solution in each nostril as needed.

Ice Pack

Ice packs are used for many ailments including, sprains, bursitis, headaches, toothache, pain, and inflammation. Ice packs also slow down bleeding and swelling. To prevent skin injury, do not hold ice directly on the skin.

Equipment:
- Ice cubes (a bag of frozen vegetables also work well).
- Plastic bag if available.
- Small towel.

Place ice cubes in the plastic bag. Fasten the end shut and wiggle bag around so that the ice lies flatly. Fold the towel around the ice pack and apply to the injured area. Leave in place for 10–30 minutes. Remove the pack and dry the moisture on the area.

Caution: Stop treatment if symptoms worsen, if there is a severe aversion to cold, or if headache occurs with ice application. Do not use if you have Raynaud's disease.

"Pleasant words are a honeycomb, sweet to the soul and healing to the bones."
—Proverbs 16:24

Physiological Effects of Hot and Cold Water Treatments

Heat	Cold
Increased blood flow	Decreased blood flow
Increased inflammatory response	Decreased inflammatory response
Increased edema production	Decreased edema production
Increased hemorrhage	Decreased hemorrhage
Decreased muscle pain & spasms	Decreased muscle pain & spasms
Decreased stiffness in arthritis	Increased stiffness in arthritis

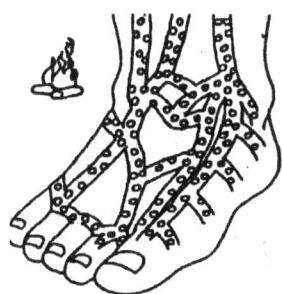 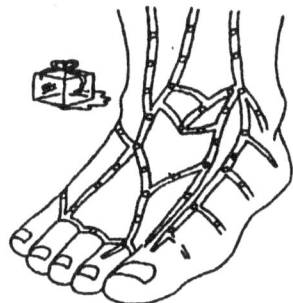

Reprinted from Clarence W. Dail, M.D. and Charles S. Thomas, Ph.D. (1985). *Simple Remedies For the Home*. Brushton, NY: TEACH Services, Inc. 19. Used by permission.

"If you don't like something, change it.
If you can't change it, change your attitude.
Don't complain."

—Maya Angelou

MISCELLANEOUS

Natural Health Websites

American Botanical Council	www.herbalgram.org
Charcoal Remedies.com	www.CharcoalRemedies.com
Health Seminars Unlimited	www.Hseminars.com
Herb Research Foundation	www.herbs.org
Lifestyle Center at Uchee Pines	www.ucheepines.org
Lifestyle Matters	www.lifestylematters.com
The Vegetarian Express	www.thevegetarianexpress.com

Resources

Herb plants and seeds:
Richter's Herbs
www.richters.com
(905) 640-6677

Baker Creek Heirloom Seeds
www.rareseeds.com
(417) 924-8917

Lip balm tubes and tubs, muslin bags, beeswax, fill-your-own tea bags, charcoal, herbs, and more:
Desert Rose Herbs
www.gmadidi@yahoo.com
(269) 781-9673

Jars and Bottles:
Mid-Continent Agrimarketing, Inc.
www.mid-conagri.com
(913) 768-8976

Burch Bottle & Packaging, Inc.
www.burchbottle.com
(518) 273-1845

Recommended Publications

Barlow, Max G. (1990). *From the Shepherd's Purse.* Hongkong: Everbest Publishing, Co.

Cooney, David O., Ph.D. *Activated Charcoal: Antidote, Remedy, and Health Aid.* Brushton, NY: TEACH Services, Inc.

Dail, Thomas W., M.D. and Charles S. Thomas, M.D. (1989). *Hydrotherapy: Simple Treatments for Common Ailments.* Brushton, NY: TEACH Services, Inc.

Dinsley, John (2005). *Charcoal Remedies.com.* Gatekeeper Books, Remnant Publications, Coldwater, MI.

Foster, Steven. (1998). *101 Medicinal Herbs.* Loveland, CO: Interweave Press.

Foster, Steven/Duke, James, (1990). *Eastern/Central Medicinal Plants.* Peterson Field Guides, Houghton Mifflin Co., New York

Hobbs, Christopher. (1998). *Handmade Medicine.* Loveland, CO: Interweave Press.

McNeilus, Mary Ann. (2001). *God's Healing Way.* Whalen, MN: Mercy Valley Farm.

Noyes, Edwin A. (2007). *Spiritualistic Deceptions in Health and Healing.* Homeward Publishing, Monrovia, CA 91017

Thrash, Calvin, M.D. and Thrash, Agatha, M.D.. (1988). *RX: Charcoal.* Benton Harbor, MI: Family Health Publications.

White, Ellen G. (1976). *Counsels on Diets & Foods.* Washington, DC: Review & Herald Publishing Association.

White, Ellen G. (1998). *The Ministry of Healing.* Coldwater, MI: Remnant Publications.

Herbal Gram. (Journal). PO Box 144345, Austin, TX 78714-4345.

Index

Breakfast
Breakfast Patties 10
Potato Cakes 10
Creole Frittata 10
Fruit Topping 11
Quick and Easy Hash Browns 11
Wonderful Waffles 12
Favorite Toast Toppings 12
Fruit Sauce 13
Rainy Day Crepes 13
French Toast 13
Hot Muesli 14
Mixed Grain Cereal 14
Great Granola 14
Scrambled Tofu 15
Hearty Breakfast Burritos 15

Breads
Squash Bread with Flaxseed 18
Rye Bread 18
Basic Whole Wheat Muffin Mix 19
Oatmeal Wheat Germ Bread 21
Whole Wheat Bread 22
Holiday Rolls 22
Pizza Dough 23
Brown Rice Bread 23
Multi-Grain Bread 24
No Oil Whole Wheat Bread 25

Spreads
Pecan Spread 26
Garbanzo Spread 26
Eggless Salad 26

Soups
Barley Soup 28
Vegetable Soup 28
Vegetable Soup II 28
Lentil and Bell Pepper Chili 29
Minestrone Soup 29
Potato Broccoli Soup 30
Chunky Potato Soup 30
Lentil Soup 30
Tomato Soup 31
Vegetarian "Chicken" Noodle Soup 31

Index

Salads

- Mediterranean Salad 34
- Raw Cranberry Relish 34
- Cucumber Dill Salad 34
- Zucchini Slaw 35
- Grandma's Potato Salad 35
- Hot or Cold Pasta Salad 35
- Southwestern Salad 36
- Vegetable Barley Salad 36
- Curried Pasta Salad 37
- Mexican Taco Salad..................... 37
- Favorite Macaroni Salad 38
- Lentil Salad 38
- Raspberry Salad 38

Vegetables

- Scalloped Potatoes 39
- Squash Casserole 39
- Baked Potatoes 39
- Creamed Curried Vegetables 40
- Black Bean Topping 40
- Spinach Patties 40
- Maple Glazed Sweet Potatoes..... 41
- Creole Soybeans 41

Main Dishes

- Jambalaya 44
- Easy Mexican Black Beans and Rice 44
- Asparagus Tofu Stir-Fry.............. 45
- Sweet Potato Veggie Stir-Fry 45
- Veggie Stir-Fry 45
- Walnut Dressing 46
- Speedy Sloppy Joes 46
- Almond Tofu Stir-Fry 46
- Basic Bread Dressing.................. 47
- Vegetarian Chili 47
- Curried Rice 48
- Spinach Calzones........................ 48
- Vegetable Curry with Rice.......... 48
- Kidney Bean Chili 49
- Spinach Rice Casserole 50
- Veggie Meatless Balls 50
- Easy Bean Casserole 51
- Rice and Bean Burritos 51
- Spinach Stuffed Shells 51
- Spinach Stuffed Shells II 52
- Vegetable Burritos 52
- Baked Beans 53
- Bean Patties 53

Soybean Patties 54

Fettuccini Alfredo........................ 54

Desserts

Cherry Almond Cookies 56

Unbaked Peanut Butter Fudge Cookies 56

Pineapple Rice Pudding.............. 56

Yellow Delicious Pie 57

Oatmeal Pie Crust 57

Unbaked Carob Brownies 58

Smoothies 58

Coconut Chip Cups..................... 58

Lemon Dessert.............................. 59

Graham Cracker Crust 59

Oatmeal Carob Cookies 60

Layered Fruit Bars 60

Pumpkin Bars 61

Heavenly Cheesecake.................. 62

Pineapple or Strawberry Tapioca.. 63

This & That

Bedda Chedda Cheese Sauce 66

Chik Seasoning 66

Freezer Spaghetti Sauce 66

Tofu Sour Cream 67

Pasta Tomato Sauce 67

Slaw Dressing 67

Thousand Island Dressing.......... 68

Nut Milk 68

Spinach Dip I 68

Spinach Dip II 69

Taco Dip.. 69

Pet Treats 70

Seasonings

Non- Irritating Seasonings......... 71

Common Irritants 76

Vegetable Seasonings 77

Cooking Times for Grains......... 79

Herbs & Natural Remedies

Introduction 82

Commonly Used Herbs 83

Glossary 88

Gathering, Drying, and Storing Herbs... 91

Index

Teas, Oils, & Syrups

Basic Herbal Tea 93
Elder Flower Tea 93
Chamomile Tea 93
Cornsilk Tea 93
Calming Tea 94
Red Clover Tea 94
Tea Pops 94
Basic Decoction 94
Milk Thistle Decoction 95
Echinacea Decoction 95
Basic Infused Herbal Oil 95
Speedy Infused Oil 96
Basic Herbal Syrup 96
Honey-Lemon Cough Syrup...... 96
Ellen's Cough Remedy 96
Elderberry Syrup 97
Honey-Lemon Cough Syrup...... 97
Elderberry Extract 98
Sore Throat Gargle 98

Baths, Poultices, Pills, Lotions & Salves

Basic Herbal Bath 99
Calming Bedtime Bath Tea 99
Oatmeal Bath 99
Herbal Poultice 100
Baby Care Tips........................... 100
Applying a Poultice 101
Onion Poultice 102
Herbal Eye Compresses 102
Easy Lip Balm 102
Herbal Compresses 103
Suggested Herbs
    for Compresses 103
Herbal Pills 104
Basic Salve Recipe..................... 104
Poison Ivy or Poison Oak
    Lotion 104

Charcoal

Cautions..................................... 105
Internal Dosages for
    Most Ailments 106
Charcoal Dosages
    for Poisoning......................... 106
Large Charcoal Poultices 107
Small Charcoal Poultices 107

Hydrotherapy

Water—To Drink....................... 108
Water—To Treat........................ 110

Hot Foot Bath 111

Heating Compress 113

Herbal Steam Inhalation 115

Steam Inhalation
  with Essential Oils 115

Chair Steam Bath or Russian
  Steam Bath Equipment 116

Saltwater Nose Drops 118

Ice Pack 118

Physiological Effects of Hot and
  Cold Water Treatments 119

Miscellaneous

Natural Health Websites 120

Resources 120

Recommended Publications 121

We invite you to view the complete
selection of titles we publish at:

www.TEACHServices.com

Scan with your mobile
device to go directly
to our website.

Please write or email us your praises, reactions, or
thoughts about this or any other book we publish at:

P.O. Box 954
Ringgold, GA 30736

info@TEACHServices.com

TEACH Services, Inc., titles may be purchased in bulk for
educational, business, fund-raising, or sales promotional use.
For information, please e-mail:

BulkSales@TEACHServices.com

Finally, if you are interested in seeing
your own book in print, please contact us at

publishing@TEACHServices.com

We would be happy to review your manuscript for free.

www.ingramcontent.com/pod-product-compliance
Lightning Source LLC
Chambersburg PA
CBHW081924170426
43200CB00014B/2818